THE FABER BOOK
OF MODERN VERSE

THE FABER BOOK
OF MODERN VERSE

edited by

MICHAEL
ROBERTS

London
FABER AND FABER
24 Russell Square

First published in February Mcmxxxvi
By Faber and Faber Limited
24 Russell Square London W.C.1
Second impression July Mcmxxxvi
Third impression February Mcmxxxvii
Fourth impression January Mcmxxxix
Fifth impression September Mcmxl
Sixth impression September Mcmxli
Seventh impression January Mcmxliii
Printed in Great Britain by
R. MacLehose and Company Limited
The University Press Glasgow
All Rights Reserved

EDITOR'S NOTE

I wish to thank those poets who have helped me in the selection and arrangement of their work. The opinions which some of them have expressed on the subject of anthologies are well known, and their collaboration in the present book does not indicate any change in that general attitude. Where the text of the poems in this book differs from that of earlier printed versions, the change has been made at the author's request.

CONTENTS

xii

INTRODUCTION

More often than prose or mathematics, poetry is received in a hostile spirit, as if its publication were an affront to the reader; yet most of the poetry which is published probably appears because, at the time of writing, it delighted the writer and convinced him that it held some profound significance or some exact description which he hoped that others, too, might see. One might expect that any poetry depending upon a very personal experience or a relatively private use of words would be ignored; and certainly a great deal of new poetry does meet with indifference because it seems private and incomprehensible. There remains, however, a considerable body of poetry which excites an active animosity, not because it states opinions and expresses feelings which are repugnant to the ordinary man, but because the reader feels compelled to argue that it is not poetry at all: many of the poems in this book aroused that animosity on their first appearance. Much of that hostility has now vanished: it is seen that these poets were saying things which were true, and important, and which could not be said as well in any other way. In that sense, it might be claimed that this collection represents the most significant poetry of this age; but the omission of Charles Sorley, Walter de la Mare, Edmund Blunden, Edwin Muir, William Plomer, Roy Campbell, all of whom seem to me to have written good poems without having been compelled to make any notable development of poetic technique, is sufficient evidence that this is not intended to be a comprehensive anthology of the best poems of our age.

The poems in the book were, with few exceptions, first printed after 1910. This date is arbitrary, and so are some of the inclusions and omissions. I have included only poems which seem to me to add to the resources of poetry, to be likely to influence the future development of poetry and language, and to please me for reasons neither personal nor idiosyncratic. But the capacity to provoke controversy has been neither a necessary nor a sufficient condition for inclusion. Mr. Yeats is included, although the breadth of his appeal has always placed him beyond controversy, but it is worth noting that in his images, approximations to ordinary speech rhythms, political implications and private references, and in his strictly poetic[1] use of myth and legend, he has anticipated many of the devices of the younger men. The earlier poems of some of the older poets are omitted, and the later included, when it is in the later work that a significant development appears. A number of young poets who have written good poems are included, although the full significance of their innovations is not yet wholly clear. Perhaps the most general characteristic of the poems in this book is that they seldom record a recognized 'poetical' experience.

To most readers it will not be surprising that an anthology of modern poetry should begin with Hopkins: but I do not mean to suggest that his poetry made a complete break with the poetry of the past and marked the inauguration of a new age. In rhythm and in imagery, as well as in the thoughts and feelings which

[1] The word 'poetic' is here used to describe a special concentration of sensuous impression, idea and evocation in a word or phrase. The word 'poetical' is used to describe an attempted evocation by conventional symbols, of a state of mind sometimes called mystical.

2

he intended to express, he differed from most of the English poets of his time, but there was no sharp discontinuity. Doughty, born only a year before Hopkins, resembled him in his inversions, his alliteration, the violence of his syntax, and above all in the emphasis which he succeeded in placing on accumulated masses of nouns, verbs, adjectives and adverbs, often unleavened by prepositions or conjunctions. Doughty's poetry is massive and uneven: a strong case could have been made out for including it; but it lacks that intensity which, in the poetry of Hopkins, was the expression of an important moral conflict, related to an outer social and intellectual conflict.

It is not possible to compile an anthology of serious poetry without reflecting the social and moral problems of our time; but writing may be poetic without being either moral or didactic. Poetry may be intended to amuse, or to ridicule, or to persuade, or to produce an effect which we feel to be more valuable than amusement and different from instruction; but primarily poetry is an exploration of the possibilities of language. It does not aim directly at consolation or moral exhortation, nor at the expression of exquisite moments, but at an extension of significance; and it might be argued that a too self-conscious concern with 'contemporary' problems deflects the poet's effort from his true objective. The technical merit of a poem is measured by its accuracy, not by the importance of a rough approximation to what is being said, nor by the number of people to whom it is immediately intelligible. If a poet is incomprehensible to many people, but clearly intelligible to a few, as Hopkins appeared to be when his collected poems were first published, it may be because he is speaking of things not commonly experi-

3

enced and is using subtleties of rhythm and imagery not used in ordinary speech, and therefore not widely understood. If it can be shown that a poet's use of language is valid for some people, we cannot dismiss his way of speaking as mere 'obscurity' and idiosyncrasy, though we may regret the necessity for such a rhetoric as we regret the necessity for scientific jargon and mathematical notation.

The significant point about Hopkins was, however, not that he invented a style different from the current poetic style, but that, working in subterranean fashion, he moulded a style which expressed the tension and disorder that he found inside himself. Good poetry is more likely to be written about subjects which are, to the writer, important, than about unimportant subjects, because only on subjects of personal importance to himself does he feel the need for that accuracy of speech which itself lessens the tension which it describes. Deliberately to imitate a style arising from one poet's crisis would be absurd, but something similar is likely to appear when a crisis of a general kind arouses a personal conflict in many poets. The conflict may be the product of a fractured personality or a decaying society, or, like some of the 'problems' of academic philosophy, a result of the deficiencies of language. The terms of the conflict may be intellectual, when people are torn between conflicting systems of ideas. They may be theological, when people argue that they themselves should be perfect, being the children of God, but are perplexed by the recognition that they are evil. The terms may be political and aesthetic, when people cling to some features of the existing state, but see that there can be no good future until that state is overthrown. Sometimes, as in Donne, several of these

4

terminologies are superimposed, serving as metaphors for each other, and concentrating, intensifying, and ultimately simplifying the problems by this poetic identification. For 'problems' of this kind are seldom independent; there is a relation between the personal and moral problem and the political and intellectual.

To those who have not felt some adumbration of such a crisis, the expression and resolution of conflict and disorder must appear like the strained muscles and distorted features of a strong man pretending to lift stupendous but non-existent weights. But for those who have come near to feeling the crisis themselves, the poetry is important. Words do something more than call up ideas and emotions out of a lumber-room: they call them up, but they never replace them exactly where they were. A good descriptive poem may enable us to be more articulate, to perceive more clearly, and to distinguish more readily between sensitive and sentimental observation, than before. But a poem may do more than that: even though we may not accept the poet's explicit doctrine, it may change the configuration of the mind and alter our responses to certain situations: it may harmonize conflicting emotions just as a good piece of reasoning may show the fallacy of an apparent contradiction in logic.

But the poetic use of language can cause discord as easily as it can cure it. A bad poem, a psychologically disordered poem, if it is technically effective may arouse uneasiness or nausea or anger in the reader. A sentimental poem, which deals with a situation by ignoring some of the factors, is offensive in this way; and a poem is equally confusing if it takes into account greater complexities of thought and intricacies of feeling than the reader has ever noticed. It unsettles the

5

mind—and by the mind I mean more than the conscious mind; and the reader expends the energy he originally brought to the poem in trivial irritation with the poet.

It is very natural that this should be the first response of many readers to 'new' poetry, but in so far as the poet is a good poet, the situation will remedy itself. The problem which worried the poet will worry other people, or the new grounds which he saw for delight and hope will become apparent to them too: perhaps their recognition of the new element will be accelerated by his writing. But in either case they will welcome the way of speech which makes them articulate. Sometimes, as in the case of Hopkins, the problem which is his today is the world's tomorrow. Sometimes his writing is significant primarily for only a few of each generation, as when it is evoked by some remote place or rare experience or an intricate thought which few can follow. Sometimes it expresses only the problem of few or many people at one particular moment. But in each case, if the writer is a good poet, good in the sense of being rhetorically effective, his writing has a value over and above that of its immediate appeal: he has added to the possibilities of speech, he has discovered evocative rhythms and image-sequences unknown before. It may happen that in some future state of society there will be no people in the position of Mr. Eliot's Prufrock, and therefore no people for whom the poem is actual. But the rhetorical merit of the poem remains: it has said something which could not be said in ordinary speech, and said it exactly, and people who are interested in effective expression will read it. Pope and Erasmus Darwin both wrote poems which were chiefly of didactic interest in their own time, but the elegance of Pope's writing keeps it alive today, whereas the poetry of Erasmus Darwin is almost forgotten. Chaucer has influenced English poetry and English language more than Langland, though Langland was, and is, the nearer to the thought and feeling of the common people.

In contrast to the previous twenty years, when the 'decadence' of the content of certain poems was continually discussed, critical discussion for the past thirty years has been concerned most often with the form, or alleged formlessness, of modern poetry. In the narrow sense, the word 'form' is used to describe special metrical and stanzaic patterns: in a wider sense it is used for the whole set of relationships involving the sensuous imagery and the auditory rhetoric of a poem. A definite 'form' in the narrower (and older) sense is not an asset unless it is an organized part of the 'form' in the wider sense, for the final value of a poem always springs from the inter-relation of form and content. In a good poet a change of development of technique always springs from a change or development of subject-matter.

If, then, we are to discuss technical innovations effectively, we must also discuss content; and here, at once, an important point appears. Roughly speaking, the poets in this book may be divided into two classes: those whose poetry is primarily a defence and vindication of existing cultural values, and those who, using the poetic qualities of the English language, try to build up poetry out of the realities implicit in the language, and which they find in their own minds rather than base it upon humanistic learning and memories of other poetry. The poets of the first kind possess what might be called a 'European' sensibility: they are aware of Baudelaire, Corbière, Rimbaud, Laforgue and the later Symbolists (it is notable that German poetry has had little influence upon them), they turn to Dante or Cavalcanti more readily than to Milton, they are more likely to be interested in a Parisian movement in poetry, such as Surrealism, than in the corresponding tendency in *Alice Through the Looking Glass* or Young's *Night Thoughts*. Most of them are Americans by birth, but their appeal is as much to the English as to the American reader. Among their English predecessors they might number Donne, Crashaw and Pope.

Poets in whose work the 'English' element predominates take the language as they find it, developing the implications of its idioms, metaphors and symbols. They are 'first order' poets: that is to say, it is not necessary to have a wide acquaintance with European literature, or even with English literature, to appreciate their work. They may be given an ancestry in Langland, Skelton, Doughty, on the one hand, and Blake, Shelley and perhaps Edward Lear, on the other, but their work does not depend upon a knowledge of literary history: it is an intensification of qualities inherent in the English language itself, and for this reason it is less easy to translate than that of the 'European' poets, in whose poems the specific properties of the language they are using is a more casual element.

These classes are not exclusive: they represent two moods of poetry rather than two kinds of poet. The poetry of W. B. Yeats, for example, must be considered under both headings: but the work of Ezra Pound and T. S. Eliot is clearly 'European' in cast. Robert Graves for a time hesitated between the two, then identified himself with that view of poetry which

8

Laura Riding has increasingly emphasized—poetry as the final residue of significance in language, freed from extrinsic decoration, superficial contemporaneity, and didactic bias.

The 'European' poet is acutely aware of the social world in which he lives, he criticizes it, but in a satirical rather than in an indignant manner, he adjusts himself to it, he is interested in its accumulated store of music, painting, sculpture, and even in its bric-à-brac. There is something of the dandy, something of the dilettante, in his make-up, but he is aware of the futility and evanescence of all this, and of the irresponsibility of big business, conventional politics and mass education. He is witty, and acutely self-conscious. His attitude is the outcome of a genuine care for much that is valuable in the past, and it gains its strength from a desire to preserve these things: to preserve them, not by violence, but by exercise, for they are not 'things' at all, but certain attitudes and activities.

Every vital age, perhaps, sees its own time as crucial and full of perils, but the problems and difficulties of our own age necessarily appear more urgent to us than those of any other, and the need for an evaluating, clarifying poetry has never been greater than it appears to be today. Industrial changes have broken up the old culture, based on an agricultural community in which poor and wealthy were alike concerned, and on a Church which bore a vital relation to the State. Parallel with this, and related to it, there has been a decay of the old moral and religious order, and a change in the basis of education, which has become more and more strictly scientific. Religion and classical learning, which once provided myths and legends symbolizing the purposes of society and the role of the individual, have declined, and the disorder weighs heavily upon the serious poet, whether in England or America.

It is the theme of many of the poems of Mr. Pound, and of Mr. Eliot's *Waste Land*. We find the American poets, Hart Crane and Allen Tate, seeing the situation in these terms:

'The Parthenon in stucco, art for the sake of death'.

And the poets—Mr. Yeats among them—have attempted to clarify their own vision by expressing the disorder which they see about them, and by finding and defining those things in the older tradition which they hold to be valuable and necessary:

Things fall apart; the centre cannot hold;
Mere anarchy is loosed upon the world,
The blood-dimmed tide is loosed, and everywhere
The ceremony of innocence is drowned;
The best lack all conviction, while the worst
Are full of passionate intensity.

If the poet is in the 'European' tradition, he describes the elements of civilization wherever he finds them: in Rome, in Greece, in Confucius, or in the Church of the Middle Ages; and against these he contrasts the violence and disorder of contemporary life. It is inevitable that poetry concerned with such issues should have political implications; but the poet is not arguing for one party against another: he is remodelling the basis upon which political creeds are founded, though sometimes immediate implications may appear in his poems.

Younger poets than Mr. Eliot and Mr. Pound may feel more acutely the inter-relation of culture and politics, but nevertheless they would agree with Mr. Auden that 'poetry is not concerned with telling people what to do, but with extending our knowledge of good and evil, perhaps making the necessity for action more urgent and its nature more clear, but only leading us to the point where it is possible for us to make a rational and moral choice'.

The problem, as we see on turning to Clough's *Amours de Voyage* (1849), is not wholly new. Clough had, as Bagehot says, 'an unusual difficulty in forming a creed as to the unseen world; he could not get the visible world out of his head; his strong grasp of plain facts and obvious matters was a difficulty to him. . . . He has himself given us in a poem, now first published, a very remarkable description of this curious state of mind. He has prefixed to it the characteristic motto, '*Il doutait de tout, même de l'amour*'. It is the delineation of a certain love-passage in the life of a hesitating young gentleman, who was in Rome at the time of the revolution of 1848; who could not make up his mind about the revolution, who could not make up his mind whether he liked Rome, who could not make up his mind whether he liked the young lady, who let her go away without him, who went in pursuit of her and could not make out which way to look for her, who, in fine, has some sort of religion but cannot tell himself what it is. . . .'

Amours de Voyage was written in conversational hexameters, in a tone of semi-satire and half-belief,

Rome disappoints me much; I hardly as yet understand, but
Rubbishy seems the word that most exactly would suit it.

Luther, they say, was unwise; like a half-taught Ger-
man, he could not

See that old follies were passing most tranquilly out
of remembrance;

Leo the Tenth was employing all efforts to clear out
abuses;

Jupiter, Juno, and Venus, Fine Arts, and Fine Letters,
the Poets,

Scholars, and Sculptors, and Painters, were quietly
clearing away the

Martyrs, and Virgins, and Saints, or at any rate
Thomas Aquinas:

He must forsooth make a fuss and distend his huge
Wittenberg lungs, and

Bring back Theology once yet again in a flood upon
Europe.

The resemblance to Mr. Pound's *Cantos*, in tone and
intention, is obvious, and there is the same detachment,
the same denial of commonly-accepted responsibility
that is found in *Mauberley* and *Prufrock*:

Dulce it is, and *decorum*, no doubt, for the country to
fall,—to

Offer one's blood an oblation to Freedom, and die
for the Cause; yet

Still, individual culture is also something. . . .

and the detachment passes easily into a kind of semi-
serious raillery, which springs from a feeling that the
generally-accepted code is all wrong, and yet that there
is no other to take its place:

Am I prepared to lay down my life for the British
female?

Really, who knows? One has bowed and talked, till,
little by little,

All the natural heat has escaped of the chivalrous
    spirit.
Oh, one conformed, of course; but one doesn't die
    for good manners,
Stab or shoot, or be shot, by way of graceful attention.
No, if it should be at all, it should be on the
    barricades there . . . .
Sooner far by the side of the damned and dirty
    plebeians.
Ah, for a child in the street I could strike; for the
    full-blown lady—
Somehow, Eustace, alas! I have not felt the vocation.

There is the same introspection, the same self-mockery
that is found in the poetry of Jules Laforgue, the same
dissatisfaction with ready-made analysis, and the same
intense conviction that there is an underlying problem
which is not to be laughed away:

I am in love, meantime, you think; no doubt you
    would think so.
I am in love, you say; with those letters, of course,
    you would say so.
I am in love, you declare. . . .
I am in love, you say: I do not think so, exactly.

There are lines which recall the more 'metaphysical'
passages of T. S. Eliot with their echoes of Chapman
and Webster:

I do not like being moved: for the will is excited; and
    action
Is a most dangerous thing; I tremble for something
    factitious,
Some malpractice of heart and illegitimate process;
We are so prone to these things, with our terrible
    notions of duty.

and there are passages of lyrical fine writing, such as we find in *The Waste Land* and the *Cantos*:

> Tibur is beautiful, too, and the orchard slopes, and
>   the Anio
> Falling, falling yet, to the ancient lyrical cadence;
> Tibur and Anio's tide; . . .

There are obvious technical resemblances (I am not denying the obvious differences) in tempo, pitch and rhythm, but Eliot and Pound differ from Clough in their greater compression and intensity. Although Clough's poem sustains its narrative interest, his hexameters, however freely handled, become irritating, and his imagery is often diffuse and unexciting. Browning and Walt Whitman, both of whom anticipated many of the habits of the modern poets, suffer from the same long-windedness. They do not compress a situation into a single memorable image, and Clough did not feel the problem of his young man as intensely as Ezra Pound and T. S. Eliot felt it in 1912. Clough suspected that the *malaise* was due to a fault in himself, and Bagehot, a sensitive critic, agreed with him; but for Pound and Eliot the problem was external: it was society and its standards that were crumbling. A culture adapted to the older aristocratic system of landed proprietors was falling to pieces in a world governed by big business. Civilization was becoming 'a few score of broken statues, an old bitch gone in the teeth' or 'a heap of broken images'. It was necessary to sift out from the mass of habits, institutions and conventions the traditions which were worth preserving.

For the moment all that the poet could do was to concentrate upon surfaces: in a world in which moral, intellectual and aesthetic values were all uncertain, only sense impressions were certain and could be described exactly. From such minute particulars perhaps something could be built up. In 1913 a few poets, shocked at the vagueness and facility of the poetry of the day, determined:

1. To use the language of common speech, but to employ always the *exact* word, not the merely decorative word.

2. To create new rhythms—as the expression of new moods. We do not insist upon 'Free-verse' as the only method of writing poetry. . . . We do believe that the individuality of a poet may often be better expressed in free verse than in conventional forms.

3. To allow absolute freedom in the choice of subject.

4. To present an image. We are not a school of painters, but we believe that poetry should render particulars exactly and not deal with vague generalities.

5. To produce poetry that is hard and clear, never blurred or indefinite.

6. Finally, most of us believe that concentration is the very essence of poetry.

Edited by Ezra Pound, a number of 'Imagist' anthologies appeared; T. E. Hulme wrote some of the earliest Imagist poems. Amy Lowell, F. S. Flint, H.D., J. G. Fletcher, Richard Aldington, T. S. Eliot and Ezra Pound himself at one time or other were members of the group, and the later development of the movement appears in the work of Marianne Moore. T. S. Eliot had been influenced by Baudelaire, Laforgue and Rimbaud. Ezra Pound was impressed by the work of

Villon and the Provençal and early Italian poets. F. S. Flint was interested in the later Symbolists—Samain, Kahn, Jammes, Rodenbach and the earlier Verhaeren —as well as more recent writers, Vildrac, Romains, Duhamel. The name 'Imagist' itself recalls 'Symbolist', and the Imagists themselves sometimes confused the image, the clear evocation of a material thing, with the symbol, the word which stirs subconscious memories. Such, indeed, was their intention: their poetry was meant to widen outwards like the ripples from a stone dropped in clear water. But the scope of 'pure' Imagist poetry was limited to clear renderings of visual experience: the poetry of H.D. shows both the possibilities and the limitations of the method.

It was natural that there should be a movement away from poeticality of subject and from the direct expression of emotion when the poets were in doubt about standards of art and morals: for the moment *any* emotion seemed sentimental to their realism. But the realism itself was often deceptive. Wallace Stevens in *The Emperor of Ice-Cream* writes a poem to insist that only the commonplace is real: let 'be' be the end of 'seem'; but the reality he describes is itself highly-coloured, and the poem contains more than a clear visual image. When he writes:

> Take from the dresser of deal,
> Lacking the three glass knobs, that sheet
> On which she embroidered fantails once
> And spread it so as to cover her face.
> If her horny feet protrude, they come
> To show how cold she is, and dumb—

I am fairly sure that he is writing with some vague memory of Mantegna's picture of the dead Christ and certainly that recollection makes the image more impressive.

The poetry of Wallace Stevens and Miss Sitwell still shows the Imagist concentration upon the sensuous surface of things, but even with the latitude which they allow themselves, Imagism is limited in scope; and as Mr. Pound has recorded: 'at a particular date in a particular room, two authors, neither engaged in picking the other's pocket, decided that the dilution of *vers libre*, Amygism, Lee Masterism, general floppiness had gone too far and that some counter-current must be set going. Parallel situation centuries ago in China. Remedy prescribed *Emaux et Cameés* (or the Bay State Hymn Book). Rhyme and regular strophes.

'Results: Poems in Mr. Eliot's *second* volume, not contained in his first *Prufrock* (Egoist, 1917), also *H. S. Mauberley*.'

Between 1920 and 1926, many poets were trying to write long poems which would present a unified view of the social crisis as they saw it, and imply their criticism of it. Conrad Aiken, who had been for a brief time influenced by the ideals of the Imagists, began to work for something which would lead to more profound and more highly organized poems, and turned to music. The predominant pattern of his poems is musical, whereas the more important pattern of some poems, as St. J. Perse's *Anabase* (translated by T. S. Eliot), is one of vivid visual and tactile images.

Conrad Aiken's *Senlin* (1918), T. S. Eliot's *The Waste Land* (1922), Richard Aldington's *Fool i' the Forest* (1925), and Archibald MacLeish's *Hamlet of A. Mac-Leish* (1928), were all poems of this kind. *The Waste Land* is the most concise, the most evocative, the widest in scope, and the most highly organized of these poems. It possesses 'imaginative order', by which I mean, that to some minds it is cogent even before its narrative and argumentative continuity is grasped. This 'imaginative order' is not something arbitrary, specific and inexplicable. If the images which are used to denote complex situations were replaced by abstractions much of the apparent incoherence of the poem would vanish. It would become a prose description of the condition of the world, a restatement of a myth and a defence of the tragic view of life. But being a poem it does more than this; a poem expresses not merely the idea of a social or scientific fact, but also the sensation of thinking or knowing, and it does not merely defend the tragic view, it may communicate it.

The images and rhythms of *The Waste Land* are not conventionally poetical: their aura of suggestion radiates from a definite meaning relating to the ordinary world, and their full significance is not seen until the essentially tragic attitude of the poem is grasped. The omission of explanatory connecting matter when contrasting a 'modern' situation with an old or the life of one class with that of another may be puzzling at first, but given a general understanding of the poem it becomes clear. Thus one situation may be described in the terms and rhythms appropriate to another, so that both the similarities and the differences are illuminated.

It is not only the 'European' poets who are concerned with these problems, nor are they the only poets who aim at poetic concentration and whose work therefore presents initial difficulties. These spring from several sources. There is the intellectual

18

difficulty which arises from the poet's use of some little-known fact, or some idea hard to grasp; there is the difficulty which comes from the unusual use of metaphor; and there is the difficulty which arises when the poet is making a deliberately fantastic use of words.

The obscurity which arises from the use of little-known or intricate ideas is easily removed. Some of the obscurity of Mr. Eliot's poetry and Mr. Empson's is of this kind: it needs only elucidatory notes to make it vanish, and it should be remembered that, because the ideas of science are widely known and generally believed, the poet who uses them is on safer ground than the man who makes classical allusions which, although they are accepted as poetical, are neither exactly appreciated nor fully understood.

The difficulty which arises from an unusual use of metaphor is less easy to remove: it depends far more upon the goodwill of the reader. Metaphor and simile are fundamental to civilized speech: but they have one serious disadvantage, the moment you say one thing is 'like' another, you remind the reader that the two things are, after all, different; and there may be an effect of dilution and long-windedness which is inimical to poetry. The poet, therefore, condenses his metaphor. Hart Crane in *Voyages III*, referring to the rhythm of the motion of a boat through a thickly clustered archipelago, speaks of 'adagios of islands'. Similarly, in *Faustus and Helen III*, the speed and altitude of an aeroplane are suggested by the idea of 'nimble blue plateaus'. This kind of compressed metaphor is also found in the poetry of Stephen Spender:

> Eye, gazelle, delicate wanderer,
> Drinker of horizon's fluid line.

This condensation may demand an initial effort of understanding in the reader, but once the meaning is understood, the aptness and convenience of the phrase is obvious; it becomes part of one's habit of thought, and the understanding of these compressed analogies becomes, after a time, no more difficult than the understanding of a simile or a more prosaic and long-winded metaphor.

The condensation of metaphor involves no denial of logic: it is simply an extension of the implications of grammar, the development of a notation which, being less cumbersome, enables us to think more easily. It may be compared to the invention of a new notation, say that of Leibnitz or Hamilton, in mathematics: the new is defined in terms of the old, it is a shorthand which must be learned by patient effort, but, once learnt, it makes possible the solution of problems which were too complicated to attack before. The human head can only carry a certain amount of notation at any one moment, and poetry takes up less space than prose.

The third difficulty, that which springs from a deliberately fantastic use of words, is less than one might imagine. We accept, willingly, the fantastic sequences of nursery-rhyme and fairy-tale; and only a confusion of thought makes us demand, as we grow older, that poetry should always give us enlightenment or high moral doctrine. The poet has a right to play, and the reader to enjoy that play. The solemn attacks on the more riotously comic of Mr. Cummings' poems are themselves ridiculous. There is in all poetry an element of verbal play; and in nonsense verses, in the poetry of Mr. Cummings, in Mr. Madge's *Lusty Juventus*, and in the early poetry of Miss Sitwell, this element often predominates. It is found in Miss Riding's *Tillaquils* which, because it actualizes a strange experience of a kind which the reader has been accustomed to regard as 'abstract', tends to be read, like her better-known poem, *The Quids*, as a satire upon academic metaphysics.

Verbal play is a form of fantasy, and when we relax and abandon ourselves to such poetry we find that some of it makes too deep an impression on our minds to be called 'play' at all. In the joke-poem we may give ourselves up to the casual association of words, but many readers find this abandonment difficult when something more serious appears to be involved. They are prepared to enjoy poetry which tells a story or states a moral, but they distrust the abandonment of common sense and accepted habits of language, believing, rightly, that if common sense is abandoned, then the way is open to all nonsense, incoherence and private fantasy.

'There is a mental existence within us . . . which is not less energetic than the conscious flow, an absent mind which haunts us like a ghost or a dream and is an essential part of our lives. Incidentally . . . the unconscious life of the mind bears a wonderful resemblance to the supposed feature of imagination. . . . To lay bare the automatic or unconscious action of the mind is indeed to unfold a tale which outvies the romances of giants and ginns, wizards in their palaces, and captives in the Domdaniel roots of the sea.'[1]

There are no rules to guide us, no histories to enable us to check our facts: but it is a simple experimental fact that certain people do agree that 'imaginative order' is found in certain specified poems, and not in

[1] E. S. Dallas, *The Gay Science* (1866).

21

others. In so far as those people are normal, it therefore seems that the poem, though 'subjective' in the old sense, is 'objective' in so far as it describes something which is part of the experience of a number of people. Poetry changes in its emphasis from one time to another, and just as, in recent years, there has been a decline in the writing of descriptive poetry (a decline which the Imagists attempted to check), so in the near future we may see greater emphasis placed on poetry as a means of appealing directly to the subconscious mind, and less on poetry as a conscious criticism of life.

As we see from the quotation from Dallas, the critical theory appropriate to such poetry is not new. Hints of its method are found in the older critics, and in Shelley. 'Poetry', said Shelley, 'differs in this respect from logic, that it is not subject to the control of the active powers of the mind, and that its birth and recurrence have no necessary connexion with the consciousness or will.' Sometimes the reason for the order of the images of such poems and the cause of their effectiveness are fairly obvious. Their power and order may come from casual memory, or from the make-up of the mind, from the deep impressions of early childhood, or from the influence of the birth trauma, or from the structure of the language itself. The meaning of a word is never a simple thing, a 'standing-for' an object or relation: it is the whole complex set of grammatical habits and associations of ideas which have grown up from our first hearing of it, and the poet exploits this symbolism of words as he exploits the more directly 'psychological' symbolism or substitution value of images. It is possible, therefore, for a poem to be professedly realistic and yet to have the vigour and insistence of a dream or nightmare. Good poetry always has something of this quality, but the nightmare may be directly verbal, rather than visual. Robert Graves is, I think, a poet whose poetry is mainly verbal. That is to say, although there is often a visual picture corresponding to his poems, the effect of the poem depends upon the direct evocative effect of the words, not on the visual stimulus.

Among the poems which deliberately free themselves from logic there are not only the joke-poems, which are simply an exercise of poetic energy showing the word-sense of the poet; but also the relaxation-poems, which range from those in which words associate themselves mainly according to relations and similarities of sound (as in Miss Sitwell's *Hornpipe*), to those which are day-dream narratives. Of these, one of the more obvious types is the wandering-ego poem in which the 'I'—'On a bat's back I do fly'— paces beside the ocean, passes through caves and dismal gorges, is prisoned in miserable dungeons, rises to craggy heights and is carried upon the wind. A poem of this kind has often a tremendous self-importance which becomes inflated until the ego dominates the entire world and we arrive at the great passages in Whitman, where, Charles Madge has pointed out, the ego passes over all the earth and eventually 'dissolves in lacy jags'.

Then again, there are the poems which, like *Kubla Khan* or, to take a modern example, Dylan Thomas's *'Light breaks where no sun shines'*, correspond to dream-fantasies of a sexual type. The woods, the hills, the rushing stream—all become substitutes for other things,

23

and the reader (and perhaps the poet), unaware of what is happening in his own mind, is puzzled at the strange excitement which he finds in the succession of images.

In some poems, the dream-quality is exaggerated and the structure which is believed to characterize the fantasies of the deeper levels in sleep is deliberately made the model for the structure of the poem. The *Parade Virtues for a Dying Gladiator* of Sacheverell Sitwell is of that kind, and so, too, are the poems which the Surrealists, and their English admirer, David Gascoyne, aim at producing. Such poems, if they are the product of a normal mind, may become fascinating when we get over their initial strangeness; but the 'order' of such poems is not necessarily identical with the 'imaginative order' of myth and legend. The poem may be a good one without being socially important, or it may be fascinating without being specifically poetic. It might, for example, be more effective as a film than it is in printed words.

But although good poems may sometimes be shown to correspond to standard types of dream, good poetry is not likely to be written by working to fit a standard pattern. Even allegory, which would seem to require constant reference to a preconceived design, cannot be written in cold blood: the writer must be interested in the story itself, not merely in the underlying 'meaning', and the story must develop with the overpowering inevitability of a dream. There are some writers who might say that if a poem has this kind of inevitability, it need not have commonsense logic or narrative sense as well. Certainly good poems of this kind have been written, though personally I prefer poems in which the compulsion of the image sequence is matched by a natural development of argument or narrative. *Kubla Khan* owes its force to its image-order, but it owes its popularity to the fact that it possesses a loose narrative order which saves the reader from the awkward fear of being taken in by nonsense. Furthermore, the two currents, the narrative and the fantastic, reinforce each other, just as the coalescence of narrative and imaginative pattern give life and force to myth and legend.

To myths, rather than to dreams, many poets still turn for the content of their poems, and the researches of Sir James Frazer and other anthropologists have provided the *motif* of a few good poems and many bad ones. Myths are more than fumbling attempts to explain historical and scientific facts: they control and organize the feeling, thought and action of a people: their function is symbolic as well as significant. But often the stories have become the conventional material of second-rate poetry, and have become perverted so that the symbolism has been lost, and we are left with the mere husk of a story, a story easily discredited by scientific and historical research. When Mr. Yeats turned to the myth as a means of giving shape and significance to his vision of the world, he was returning to the essential purpose of the myth and setting an example which Mr. Eliot, among others, has followed. But the modern reader cannot be expected to be influenced by a myth whose plain narrative sense is counter to his everyday beliefs. Either the poet must break away from any such direct narrative, or he must attempt, as I think Mr. Day Lewis has attempted in his *Flight* poem, to present a story credible in the ordinary everyday sense. If the poet turns to an existing myth or legend, however shop-soiled, and sees in it a profound significance, he will see the legend itself exemplified and symbolized in the world about him.

'So', says Hart Crane, in an unpublished manuscript, 'I found "Helen" sitting in a street car; the Dionysian revels of her court and her seduction were transferred to a Metropolitan roof garden with a jazz orchestra: and the *katharsis* of the fall of Troy I saw approximated in the recent world war. . . .

'It is a terrific problem that faces the poet today—a world that is so in transition from a decayed culture toward a reorganization of human evaluations that there are few common terms, general denominators of speech, that are solid enough or that ring with any vibration or spiritual conviction. The great mythologies of the past (including the Church) are deprived of enough façade even to launch good raillery against. Yet much of their traditions are operative still—in millions of chance combinations of related and unrelated detail, psychological reference, figures of speech, precepts, etc. These are all part of our common experience and the terms, at least partially, of that very experience when it defines or extends itself.

'The deliberate program, then, of a "break" with the past or tradition seems to me to be a sentimental fallacy. . . . The poet has a right to draw on whatever practical resources he finds in books or otherwise about him. He must tax his sensibility and his touchstone of experience for the proper selections of these themes and details, however,—and that is where he either stands, or falls into useless archaeology.

'I put no particular value on the simple objective of "modernity". . . . It seems to me that a poet will accidentally define his time well enough simply by reacting honestly and to the full extent of his sensi-

26

bilities to the states of passion, experience and rumina-
tion that fate forces on him, first hand. He must, of
course, have a sufficiently universal basis of experience
to make his imagination selective and valuable. . . .

'I am concerned with the future of America . . . be-
cause I feel persuaded that here are destined to be dis-
covered certain as yet undefined spiritual quantities,
perhaps a new hierarchy of faith not to be developed so
completely elsewhere. And in this process I like to feel
myself as a potential factor; certainly I must speak in
its terms. . . .

'But to fool one's self that definitions are being
reached by merely referring frequently to skyscrapers,
radio antennae, steam whistles, or other surface pheno-
mena of our time is merely to paint a photograph. I
think that what is interesting and significant will
emerge only under the conditions of our submission to,
and examination and assimilation of the organic effects
on us of these and other fundamental factors of our
experience. It can certainly not be an organic expres-
sion otherwise. And the expression of such values may
often be as well accomplished with the vocabulary and
blank verse of the Elizabethans as with the calligraphic
tricks and slang used so brilliantly at times by an
impressionist like Cummings.'

If a poet is to give new life to a legend, if indeed he
is to write good poetry at all, he must charge each
word to its maximum poetic value. It must appeal
concurrently to all the various levels of evocation
and interpretation: experiments in new rhythms and
new images, if they are not used in this specifically
poetic way, are of no more than technical interest. In
discussing new technical devices a distinction must be

drawn between those which produce an effect upon the reader even before he has noticed them, and those which, like some of the devices of Mr. Cummings, attract the reader's attention and lead him to infer, by ordinary reasoning, what effect the poet intended to produce. There are, I think, many examples of the first kind in this book, and of the many auditory devices of this kind, none, perhaps, are more effective, or have had greater effect upon later poets, than those of Wilfred Owen.

In Owen's poetry, the use of half-rhymes is not merely the result of an attempt to escape from the over-obviousness of rhyme-led poetry, though Owen probably discovered its possibilities in that way. His innovations are important because his sound-effects directly reinforce the general effect which he is trying to produce. In Owen's war poetry, the half-rhymes almost invariably fall from a vowel of high pitch to one of low pitch, producing an effect of frustration, disappointment, hopelessness. In other poets, rising half-rhymes are used, which produce the opposite effect, without reaching out to the full heartiness of rhyme. Full end-rhyme itself is felt by many modern poets to be too arbitrary and too noisy for serious poetry, unless modified, as Hopkins modifies it, by taking some of the stress off the last syllable of the line either by stressing earlier syllables, or by placing the emphasis of meaning, as distinct from metre, elsewhere. If they use end-rhymes at all, it is often for satiric purposes, or in a modified form, rhyming stressed with unstressed syllables, as Sacheverell Sitwell has done, and thus producing an uncertain, tentative, hesitating effect in keeping with the poet's purpose.

Nevertheless rhyme, like meaning and metre, is one of the possible elements in a verbal pattern, and few poets abandon it entirely. The sense of order in complication is part of the fascination of poetry, and often, as in the poetry of C. Day Lewis, internal rhymes, carefully but not obviously placed, are used to produce a pattern running counter to sense and rhythm and to add that intricacy and richness which marks the difference between part-song and unison.

Even when the poet writes, apparently, in a regular metre, he may use effects ignored in the formal rules of prosody and grammar. Thus Owen, in the second stanza of *Futility*, retards the movement of the first four lines by punctuation and intricacy of syntax, so that the fifth line, unimpeded, comes out with a terrific force, continued, though less vigorously and a little more slowly, as though one added a conclusive after-thought, in the final couplet. Similarly, in William Empson's *Note on Local Flora* the first seven lines form a single intricate sentence, retarding the pace, so that the eighth line, again an unimpeded sentence, is stamped with the emphasis of conviction, and the con-cluding couplet comes strongly, but comparatively quietly, as a conclusive deduction might do.

Often an effect of logic in a poem which, when ex-amined, proves illogical, is due to auditory rhetoric[1] rather than to fantasy. The poetry of Edith and Sache-verell Sitwell shows, for example, not only an unusually vivid use of sensuous impressions, and of image-patterns based, like nursery rhymes, on the compelling

[1] I use the word 'rhetoric' here, as elsewhere, in the technical, not the popular sense. There is good rhetoric and bad rhetoric, and there is rhetoric used in a good cause and in a bad, but rhetoric itself is not necessarily bad.

force of dreams, but also an effective use of sound-patterns having this convincing facility of speech. The poetry of Edith Sitwell, like the poetry of Vachel Lindsay and E. E. Cummings, needs to be read aloud, with careful changes of rhythm, volume, pitch and tempo. A practised reader will be able to determine these variations for himself: in a good poem they are usually implied, but the pointing of the Psalms is an example of the use of typography to help the reader. Similarly, Hopkins, in his effort to extract the utmost poetic value from the varied stress of words, resorts to a system of accents and markings; and Mr. Cummings takes a great deal of trouble to show, by typographical devices, how his poems should be read. More conventional poets are less violent in their fluctuations, and less helpful in their methods. To read poetry as it should be read requires considerable practice. Most people tend to overemphasize any regular metrical pattern which may be the background to the rhythm of the poem, and at the same time they raise the voice to a deliberately 'poetical' key and make use of fluctuations of pitch which bring their reading nearer to singing than to talking. It is characteristic of modern poets in general that they fight as hard as they can against this tendency, which seems to them not to increase the significance of the poetry, but to diminish it by asserting an arbitrary music at the expense of meaning, and to read their poems as songs, and necessarily bad songs, is to misread them completely.

When in pre-war days a few poets began to write, not in regular metres, but in cadences, as Whitman and the translators of the Bible had done, it was objected that this practice would destroy the art of verse entirely. It is true that a more delicate sensibility and a more careful training are necessary if we are to appreciate cadenced verse, and it is true that the existence of cadenced verse blurs the distinction between prose and poetry; but the critical vocabulary must be revised to fit the facts: to deny the facts and close your ears to the rhythms is to behave like the Inquisitor who refused to look through Galileo's telescope. Every discovery creates disorder: it is not the duty of the critic to prevent discovery or to deny it, but to create new order to replace the older. Today, the quarrel over cadenced verse has died down, and it is very hard to draw a sharp line, or to see any purpose in trying to draw a sharp line, between 'free' verse and *varied* regular verse. One or two points may be noted, however. There is verse which is intended to be 'free': that is to say, whose rhythm is composed to please the ear alone; there is verse which is quantitative, depending on a recurrent pattern of long and short syllables; there is verse which is accentual, depending on a recurrent pattern of accented and unaccented syllables; and there is syllabic verse. In the latter (some of the poems of Marianne Moore and Herbert Read are examples) the lines are evaluated by the number of syllables they contain, and the pattern will be something like this—11:11:11:6. It is not very difficult to train the ear to recognize and enjoy syllabic patterns, and if it is objected that this training is 'unnatural' it must be pointed out that all training is 'unnatural' and yet inevitable. Even the writer of 'free' verse has been trained to enjoy and detect certain patterns, and his 'free' verse often shows the skeleton of a 'regular' pattern underneath.

These effects are not felt by every reader: to some,

the devices are merely evidence of technical incompetence. It is, however, demonstrable that some people respond to them without having them pointed out; the only possible conclusion is that these people are more sensitive to language than the others. The only objection to such devices is that it would never be possible to teach everyone to respond to them, therefore they tend to cut off one section of the community from another. But the same objection could be brought against the theory of tensors, and it is as necessary that some members of the community should explore the possibilities of language and use it to control and clarify emotional, spiritual and sensuous experience, as it is that others should use their mathematical notation to codify and organize our scientific knowledge.

Modern poets have been decreasingly concerned with sound-effects as independent entities, and today the auditory rhetoric of poetry is dictated, not by its own rules, but by the central impulse of the poem. Perhaps for this reason, no adequate study of auditory rhetoric exists. Prosody is little more than an enumeration and naming of all the possible combinations of stressed and unstressed syllables. It takes no account of the variety of stresses, or of the quantitative patterns interwoven with accentual patterns, and it ignores the 'laws' of consonant and vowel sequences. It becomes useless if it loses sight of its original purpose and erects itself into a system of unchanging orthodoxy. In criticism all general rules and classifications are elucidatory: and new discoveries or the introduction of matters previously thought to be irrelevant may compel us to amend them or admit their limitations.

The critic tries to make distinctions and to discover rules valid for the widest possible variety of purpose; but for different purposes different classifications may be necessary, and this is true not only of the classifications which we use in discussing the technique of poetry, but also of those which we use when speaking of the poets. Where, as in the criticism of poetry, we are dealing with something as complex as personalities, any division must be arbitrary. An historical or categorical label never prescribes the ultimate achievements of the poet, it merely tells us where to look for them; and from time to time, if we are to recognize the poet as a mobile force, new categories are needed.

Often the new dividing line between the categories may not be far removed from the old; and it may be objected that the classification which results from a distinction between the 'English' sensibility and 'European' sensibility does not differ very much from the distinction between 'romantic' and 'classic' writers, or between 'pure' poetry and 'didactic and descriptive' poetry. There is, however, a difference in the points on which it focusses our attention. Any distinction in terms of schools and tendencies is misleading if we use it for any purpose beyond concentrating our attention for a moment on one aspect of the work of one or two selected writers; and if for the moment I have classified poets, it is merely as a shop-window arrangement, a tactful use of contrasts to focus attention on certain qualities, and to lessen some of the difficulty which readers find when they approach modern poetry for the first time.

New poetry is never popular unless it accepts the prejudices of the immediate past, and, giving an aura of heroism to actions which are already inevitable, stifles those misgivings out of which the real decisions of the present are to grow. Often in reading poems for this anthology, I have come upon one which, though its beginning seemed to show an apprehension beyond the commonplace, lapsed at the end into a false simplicity: a statement in familiar terms which had been given no new significance and depth. I have found Mr. Aldington's poems, in spite of their innovations, disappointing in that way; the earlier poems of Mr. Monro, and many of the poems of Mr. Cummings affect me similarly. The poet has seen something, and almost seen it clearly; and then at the end, unable to say it, he has been content to say some lesser thing, and the true poem remains unwritten.

For a time, the false poem may be more popular than the true one could have been. 'The poet', Johnson said, 'must divest himself of the prejudice of his age and country; he must consider right and wrong in their abstracted and invariable state; he must disregard present laws and opinions, and rise to general and transcendental truths, which will always be the same. He must, therefore, content himself with the slow progress of his name, contemn the praise of his own time, and commit his claims to the justice of posterity.'

Sometimes it is argued that readers, too, must leave the judgment of contemporary literature to posterity; but the judgment of posterity is only another name for the accumulated judgments of those who read most carefully and with least prejudice and preconception. To read merely to concur in the judgments of our ancestors is to inhibit all spontaneous response and to miss the pleasure of that reading which moulds the opinions, tastes and actions of our time. The first important thing about contemporary literature is that it *is* contemporary: it is speaking to us and for us, here, now. Judgment can only follow an act of sympathy and understanding, and to let our appreciation grow outwards from that which immediately appeals to us is both wiser and more enjoyable than to echo the judgments of others or to restrict and sour our appreciation by hastily attacking anything which at first seems difficult or irritating.

POETRY

GERARD MANLEY HOPKINS

THE WRECK OF THE DEUTSCHLAND

To the
happy memory of five Franciscan Nuns
exiles by the Falk Laws
drowned between midnight and morning of
Dec. 7th, 1875

PART THE FIRST

1

Thou mastering me
God! giver of breath and bread;
World's strand, sway of the sea;
Lord of living and dead;
Thou hast bound bones and veins in me, fastened me
flesh,
And after it almost unmade, what with dread,
Thy doing: and dost thou touch me afresh?
Over again I feel thy finger and find thee.

2

I did say yes
O at lightning and lashed rod;
Thou heardst me truer than tongue confess
Thy terror, O Christ, O God;
Thou knowest the walls, altar and hour and night:
The swoon of a heart that the sweep and the hurl of
thee trod
Hard down with a horror of height:
And the midriff astrain with leaning of, laced with fire
of stress.

39

3

The frown of his face
Before me, the hurtle of hell
Behind, where, where was a, where was a place?
I whirled out wings that spell
And fled with a fling of the heart to the heart of the
Host.
My heart, but you were dovewinged, I can tell,
Carrier-witted, I am bold to boast,
To flash from the flame to the flame then, tower from
the grace to the grace.

4

I am soft sift
In an hourglass—at the wall
Fast, but mined with a motion, a drift,
And it crowds and it combs to the fall;
I steady as a water in a well, to a poise, to a pane,
But roped with, always, all the way down from the
tall
Fells or flanks of the voel, a vein
Of the gospel proffer, a pressure, a principle, Christ's
gift.

5

I kiss my hand
To the stars, lovely-asunder
Starlight, wafting him out of it; and
Glow, glory in thunder;
Kiss my hand to the dappled-with-damson west:
Since, tho' he is under the world's splendour and
wonder,
His mystery must be instressed, stressed;

For I greet him the days I meet him, and bless when I
understand.

GERARD
MANLEY
HOPKINS

6

Not out of his bliss
Springs the stress felt
Nor first from heaven (and few know this)
Swings the stroke dealt—
Stroke and a stress that stars and storms deliver,
That guilt is hushed by, hearts are flushed by and
melt—
But it rides time like riding a river
(And here the faithful waver, the faithless fable and
miss).

7

It dates from day
Of his going in Galilee;
Warm-laid grave of a womb-life grey;
Manger, maiden's knee;
The dense and the driven Passion, and frightful
sweat;
Thence the discharge of it, there its swelling to be,
Though felt before, though in high flood yet—
What none would have known of it, only the heart,
being hard at bay.

8

Is out with it! Oh,
We lash with the best or worst
Word last! How a lush-kept plush-capped sloe
Will, mouthed to flesh-burst,
Gush!—flush the man, the being with it, sour or
sweet,

41

Brim, in a flash, full!—Hither then, last or first,
To hero of Calvary, Christ's feet—
Never ask if meaning it, wanting it, warned of it—men
go.

9

Be adored among men,
God, three-numberèd form;
Wring thy rebel, dogged in den,
Man's malice, with wrecking and storm.
Beyond saying sweet, past telling of tongue,
Thou art lightning and love, I found it, a winter and
warm;
Father and fondler of heart thou hast wrung:
Hast thy dark descending and most art merciful then.

10

With an anvil-ding
And with fire in him forge thy will
Or rather, rather then, stealing as Spring
Through him, melt him but master him still:
Whether at once, as once at a crash Paul,
Or as Austin, a lingering-out sweet skill,
Make mercy in all of us, out of us all
Mastery, but be adored, but be adored King.

PART THE SECOND

11

'Some find me a sword; some
The flange and the rail; flame,
Fang, or flood' goes Death on drum,
And storms bugle his fame.

42

But wé dream we are rooted in earth—Dust!
  Flesh falls within sight of us, we, though our flower the same,
    Wave with the meadow, forget that there must
The sour scythe cringe, and the blear share come.

GERARD
MANLEY
HOPKINS

12

    On Saturday sailed from Bremen,
      American-outward-bound,
      Take settler and seamen, tell men with women,
        Two hundred souls in the round—
O Father, not under thy feathers nor ever as guess-
        ing
The goal was a shoal, of a fourth the doom to be
        drowned;
    Yet did the dark side of the bay of thy blessing
Not vault them, the millions of rounds of thy mercy
        not reeve even them in?

13

    Into the snows she sweeps,
      Hurling the haven behind,
    The Deutschland, on Sunday; and so the sky
        keeps,
      For the infinite air is unkind,
And the sea flint-flake, black-backed in the regular
        blow,
    Sitting Eastnortheast, in cursed quarter, the wind;
    Wiry and white-fiery and whirlwind-swivellèd
        snow
Spins to the widow-making unchilding unfathering
        deeps.

She drove in the dark to leeward,
She struck—not a reef or a rock
But the combs of a smother of sand: night drew
her
Dead to the Kentish Knock;
And she beat the bank down with her bows and the
ride of her keel:
The breakers rolled on her beam with ruinous
shock;
And canvas and compass, the whorl and the wheel
Idle for ever to waft her or wind her with, these she
endured.

15

Hope had grown grey hairs,
Hope had mourning on,
Trenched with tears, carved with cares,
Hope was twelve hours gone;
And frightful a nightfall folded rueful a day
Nor rescue, only rocket and lightship, shone,
And lives at last were washing away:
To the shrouds they took,—they shook in the hurling
and horrible airs.

16

One stirred from the rigging to save
The wild woman-kind below,
With a rope's end round the man, handy and
brave—
He was pitched to his death at a blow,
For all his dreadnought breast and braids of thew:
They could tell him for hours, dandled the to and fro

Through the cobbled foam-fleece, what could he do GERARD
With the burl of the fountains of air, buck and the   MANLEY
        flood of the wave?   HOPKINS

17

    They fought with God's cold—
    And they could not and fell to the deck
    (Crushed them) or water (and drowned them) or
        rolled
    With the sea-romp over the wreck.
Night roared, with the heart-break hearing a heart-
        broke rabble,
The woman's wailing, the crying of child without
        check—
    Till a lioness arose breasting the babble,
A prophetess towered in the tumult, a virginal tongue
        told.

18

    Ah, touched in your bower of bone
    Are you! turned for an exquisite smart,
    Have you! make words break from me here all
        alone,
    Do you!—mother of being in me, heart.
O unteachably after evil, but uttering truth,
Why, tears! is it? tears; such a melting, a madrigal
        start!
    Never-eldering revel and river of youth,
What can it be, this glee? the good you have there of
        your own?

19

    Sister, a sister calling
    A master, her master and mine!—

45

And the inboard seas run swirling and hawling;
        The rash smart sloggering brine
    Blinds her; but she that weather sees one thing, one;
    Has one fetch in her: she rears herself to divine
        Ears, and the call of the tall nun
    To the men in the tops and the tackle rode over the
            storm's brawling.

20

        She was first of a five and came
            Of a coifèd sisterhood.
        (O Deutschland, double a desperate name!
            O world wide of its good!
    But Gertrude, lily, and Luther, are two of a town,
        Christ's lily and beast of the waste wood:
            From life's dawn it is drawn down,
    Abel is Cain's brother and breasts they have sucked the
            same.)

21

        Loathed for a love men knew in them,
            Banned by the land of their birth,
        Rhine refused them. Thames would ruin them;
            Surf, snow, river and earth
    Gnashed: but thou art above, thou Orion of light;
        Thy unchancelling poising palms were weighing the
            worth,
            Thou martyr-master: in thy sight
    Storm flakes were scroll-leaved flowers, lily showers—
            sweet heaven was astrew in them.

22

        Five! the finding and sake
            And cipher of suffering Christ.

Mark, the mark is of man's make
   And the word of it Sacrificed.
But he scores it in scarlet himself on his own be-
      spoken,
   Before-time-taken, dearest prizèd and priced—
   Stigma, signal, cinquefoil token
For lettering of the lamb's fleece, ruddying of the-rose
   flake.

GERARD
MANLEY
HOPKINS

23

   Joy fall to thee, father Francis,
   Drawn to the Life that died;
With the gnarls of the nails in thee, niche of the
      lance, his
   Lovescape crucified
And seal of his seraph-arrival! and these thy
      daughters
   And five-livèd and leavèd favour and pride,
   Are sisterly sealed in wild waters,
To bathe in his fall-gold mercies, to breathe in his all-
   fire glances.

24

   Away in the loveable west,
   On a pastoral forehead of Wales,
I was under a roof here, I was at rest,
   And they the prey of the gales;
She to the black-about air, to the breaker, the
      thickly
Falling flakes, to the throng that catches and quails
   Was calling 'O Christ, Christ, come quickly':
The cross to her she calls Christ to her, christens her
   wild-worst Best.

The majesty! what did she mean?
Breathe, arch and original Breath.
Is it love in her of the being as her lover had been?
Breathe, body of lovely Death.
They were else-minded then, altogether, the men
Woke thee with a *we are perishing* in the weather of
Gennesareth.
Or is it that she cried for the crown then,
The keener to come at the comfort for feeling the
combating keen?

26

For how to the heart's cheering
The down-dugged ground-hugged grey
Hovers off, the jay-blue heavens appearing
Of pied and peeled May!
Blue-beating and hoary-glow height; or night, still
higher,
With belled fire and the moth-soft Milky Way,
What by your measure is the heaven of desire,
The treasure never eyesight got, nor was ever guessed
what for the hearing?

27

No, but it was not these.
The jading and jar of the cart,
Time's tasking, it is fathers that asking for ease
Of the sodden-with-its-sorrowing heart,
Not danger, electrical horror; then further it finds
The appealing of the Passion is tenderer in prayer
apart:

Other, I gather, in measure her mind's
Burden, in wind's burly and beat of endragonèd seas.

28

But how shall I . . . make me room there:
Reach me a . . . Fancy, come faster—
Strike you the sight of it? look at it loom there,
Thing that she . . . there then! the Master,
Ipse, the only one, Christ, King, Head:
He was to cure the extremity where he had cast her;
Do, deal, lord it with living and dead;
Let him ride, her pride, in his triumph, despatch and
have done with his doom there.

29

Ah! there was a heart right!
There was single eye!
Read the unshapeable shock night
And knew the who and the why;
Wording it how but by him that present and past,
Heaven and earth are word of, worded by?—
The Simon Peter of a soul! to the blast
Tarpeian-fast, but a blown beacon of light.

30

Jesu, heart's light,
Jesu, maid's son,
What was the feast followed the night
Thou hadst glory of this nun?—
Feast of the one woman without stain.
For so conceivèd, so to conceive thee is done;
But here was heart-throe, birth of a brain,
Word, that heard and kept thee and uttered thee out-
right.

Well, she has thee for the pain, for the
Patience; but pity of the rest of them!
Heart, go and bleed at a bitterer vein for the
Comfortless unconfessed of them—
No not uncomforted: lovely-felicitous Providence
Finger of a tender of, O of a feathery delicacy, the
breast of the
Maiden could obey so, be a bell to, ring of it, and
Startle the poor sheep back! is the shipwrack then a
harvest, does tempest carry the grain
for thee?

32

I admire thee, master of the tides,
Of the Yore-flood, of the year's fall;
The recurb and the recovery of the gulf's sides,
The girth of it and the wharf of it and the wall;
Stanching, quenching ocean of a motionable mind;
Ground of being, and granite of it: past all
Grasp God, throned behind
Death with a sovereignty that heeds but hides, bodes
but abides;

33

With a mercy that outrides
The all of water, an ark
For the listener; for the lingerer with a love
glides
Lower than death and the dark;
A vein for the visiting of the past-prayer, pent in
prison,
The-last-breath penitent spirits—the uttermost
mark

Our passion-plungèd giant risen,
The Christ of the Father compassionate, fetched in the
storm of his strides.

GERARD
MANLEY
HOPKINS

34

Now burn, new born to the world,
Double-naturèd name,
The heaven-flung, heart-fleshed, maiden-furled
Miracle-in-Mary-of-flame,
Mid-numbered He in three of the thunder-throne!
Not a dooms-day dazzle in his coming nor dark as he
came;
Kind, but royally reclaiming his own;
A released shower, let flash to the shire, not a lightning
of fire hard-hurled.

35

Dame, at our door
Drowned, and among our shoals,
Remember us in the roads, the heaven-haven of
the Reward:
Our King back, oh, upon English souls!
Let him easter in us, be a dayspring to the dimness
of us, be a crimson-cresseted east,
More brightening her, rare-dear Britain, as his reign
rolls,
Pride, rose, prince, hero of us, high-priest,
Our hearts' charity's hearth's fire, our thoughts'
chivalry's throng's Lord.

GERARD
MANLEY
HOPKINS

Felix Randal the farrier, O he is dead then? my duty
    all ended,
Who have watched his mould of man, big-boned and
    hardy-handsome
Pining, pining, till time when reason rambled in it and
    some
Fatal four disorders, fleshed there, all contended?

Sickness broke him. Impatient he cursed at first, but
    mended
Being anointed and all; though a heavenlier heart began
    some
Months earlier, since I had our sweet reprieve and
    ransom
Tendered to him. Ah well, God rest him all road ever
    he offended!

This seeing the sick endears them to us, us too it en-
    dears.
My tongue had taught thee comfort, touch had
    quenched thy tears,
Thy tears that touched my heart, child, Felix, poor
    Felix Randal;

How far from then forethought of, all thy more
    boisterous years,
When thou at the random grim forge, powerful amidst
    peers,
Didst fettle for the great grey drayhorse his bright and
    battering sandal!

PIED BEAUTY

GERARD
MANLEY
HOPKINS

Glory be to God for dappled things—
 For skies of couple-colour as a brinded cow;
  For rose-moles all in stipple upon trout that swim;
Fresh-firecoal chestnut-falls; finches' wings;
 Landscape plotted and pieced—fold, fallow, and
    plough;
  And áll trádes, their gear and tackle and trim.

All things counter, original, spare, strange;
 Whatever is fickle, freckled (who knows how?)
  With swift, slow; sweet, sour; adazzle, dim;
He fathers-forth whose beauty is past change:
    Praise him.

ANDROMEDA

Now Time's Andromeda on this rock rude,
With not her either beauty's equal or
Her injury's, looks off by both horns of shore,
Her flower, her piece of being, doomed dragon's food.
 Time past she has been attempted and pursued
By many blows and banes; but now hears roar
A wilder beast from West than all were, more
Rife in her wrongs, more lawless, and more lewd.

 Her Perseus linger and leave her tó her extremes?—
Pillowy air he treads a time and hangs
His thoughts on her, forsaken that she seems,
 All while her patience, morselled into pangs,
Mounts; then to alight disarming, no one dreams,
With Gorgon's gear and barebill, thongs and fangs.

GERARD
MANLEY
HOPKINS
THE CANDLE INDOORS

Some candle clear burns somewhere I come by.
I muse at how its being puts blissful back
With yellowy moisture mild night's blear-all black,
Or to-fro tender trambeams truckle at the eye.
By that window what task what fingers ply,
I plod wondering, a-wanting, just for lack
Of answer the eagerer a-wanting Jessy or Jack
There—God to aggrándise, God to glorify.—

Come you indoors, come home; your fading fire
Mend first and vital candle in close heart's vault:
You there are master, do your own desire;
What hinders? Are you beam-blind, yet to a fault
In a neighbour deft-handed? are you that liar
And, cast by conscience out, spendsavour salt?

INVERSNAID

This darksome burn, horseback brown,
His rollrock highroad roaring down,
In coop and in comb the fleece of his foam
Flutes and low to the lake falls home.

A windpuff-bonnet of fáwn-fróth
Turns and twindles over the broth
Of a pool so pitchblack, féll-frówning,
It rounds and rounds Despair to drowning.

Degged with dew, dappled with dew
Are the groins of the braes that the brook treads
　　　through,

54

Wiry heathpacks, flitches of fern,
And the beadbonny ash that sits over the burn.

What would the world be, once bereft
Of wet and of wildness? Let them be left,
O let them be left, wildness and wet;
Long live the weeds and the wilderness yet.

GERARD
MANLEY
HOPKINS

THE WINDHOVER:

To Christ our Lord

I caught this morning morning's minion, king-
dom of daylight's dauphin, dapple-dawn-drawn
Falcon, in his riding
Of the rolling level underneath him steady air, and
striding
High there, how he rung upon the rein of a wimpling
wing
In his ecstasy! then off, off forth on swing,
As a skate's heel sweeps smooth on a bow-bend: the
hurl and gliding
Rebuffed the big wind. My heart in hiding
Stirred for a bird,—the achieve of, the mastery of the
thing!

Brute beauty and valour and act, oh, air, pride, plume,
here
Buckle! AND the fire that breaks from thee then, a
billion
Times told lovelier, more dangerous, O my chevalier!

No wonder of it: shéer plód makes plough down
sillion
Shine, and blue-bleak embers, ah my dear,
Fall, gall themselves, and gash gold-vermilion.

'AS KINGFISHERS CATCH FIRE, DRAGON-FLIES DRAW FLAME'

As kingfishers catch fire, dragonflies dráw fláme;
As tumbled over rim in roundy wells
Stones ring; like each tucked string tells, each hung
    bell's
Bow swung finds tongue to fling out broad its name;
Each mortal thing does one thing and the same:
Deals out that being indoors each one dwells;
Selves—goes itself; *myself* it speaks and spells,
Crying *Whát I do is me: for that I came.*

Í say móre: the just man justices;
Kéeps gráce: thát keeps all his goings graces;
Acts in God's eye what in God's eye he is—
Chríst—for Christ plays in ten thousand places,
Lovely in limbs, and lovely in eyes not his
To the Father through the features of men's faces.

HARRY PLOUGHMAN

Hard as hurdle arms, with a broth of goldish flue
Breathed round; the rack of ribs; the scooped flank;
    lank
Rope-over thigh; knee-nave; and barrelled shank—
        Head and foot, shoulder and shank—
By a grey eye's heed steered well, one crew, fall to;
Stand at stress. Each limb's barrowy brawn, his thew
That onewhere curded, onewhere sucked or sank—
        Soared or sank—,
Though as a beechbole firm, finds his, as at a roll-call,
    rank
And features, in flesh, what deed he each must do—
        His sinew-service where do.

He leans to it, Harry bends, look. Back, elbow, and
     liquid waist
In him, all quail to the wallowing o' the plough: GERARD
MANLEY
HOPKINS
     's cheek crimsons; curls
Wag or crossbridle, in a wind lifted, windlaced—
          See his wind- lilylocks-laced;
Churlsgrace, too, child of Amansstrength, how it hangs
     or hurls
Them—broad in bluff hide his frowning feet lashed!
     raced
With, along them, cragiron under and cold furls—
          With-a-fountain's shining-shot furls.

'NO WORST, THERE IS NONE. PITCHED PAST PITCH OF GRIEF'

No worst, there is none. Pitched past pitch of grief,
More pangs will, schooled at forepangs, wilder wring.
Comforter, where, where is your comforting?
Mary, mother of us, where is your relief?
My cries heave, herds-long; huddle in a main, a chief
Woe, world-sorrow; on an age-old anvil wince and
     sing—
Then lull, then leave off. Fury had shrieked 'No ling-
ering! Let me be fell: force I must be brief'.

  O the mind, mind has mountains; cliffs of fall
Frightful, sheer, no-man-fathomed. Hold them cheap
May who ne'er hung there. Nor does long our small
Durance deal with that steep or deep. Here! creep,
Wretch, under a comfort serves in a whirlwind: all
Life death does end and each day dies with sleep.

SPELT FROM SIBYL'S LEAVES

Earnest, earthless, equal, attuneable, | vaulty, vol-
uminous, . . . stupendous

Evening strains to be tíme's vást, | womb-of-all, home
of-all, hearse-of-all night.

Her fond yellow hornlight wound to the west, | her
wild hollow hoarlight hung to the height

Waste; her earliest stars, earl-stars, | stárs principal,
overbend us,

Fíre-féaturing heaven. For earth | her being has un-
bound, her dapple is at an end, as-

tray or aswarm, all throughther, in throngs; | self ín
self steepèd and páshed—qúite

Disremembering, dísmémbering | áll now. Heart,
you round me right

With: Óur évening is over us; óur night | whélms,
whélms, ánd will end us.

Only the beak-leaved boughs dragonish | damask the
tool-smooth bleak light; black,

Ever so black on it. Óur tale, O óur oracle! | Lét life,
wáned, ah lét life wind

Off hér once skéined stained véined varíety | upon, áll
on twó spools; párt, pen, páck

Now her áll in twó flocks, twó folds—black, white; |
right, wrong; reckon but, reck but, mind

But thése two; wáre of a wórld where bút these | twó
tell, each off the óther; of a rack

Where, selfwrung, selfstrung, sheathe- and shelterless,
thóughts agaínst thoughts ín groans grínd.

'MY OWN HEART LET ME MORE HAVE PITY ON; LET'

GERARD
MANLEY
HOPKINS

My own heart let me more have pity on; let
Me live to my sad self hereafter kind,
Charitable; not live this tormented mind
With this tormented mind tormenting yet.
　　I cast for comfort I can no more get
By groping round my comfortless, than blind
Eyes in their dark can day or thirst can find
Thirst's all-in-all in all a world of wet.

　　Soul, self; come, poor Jackself, I do advise
You, jaded, let be; call off thoughts awhile
Elsewhere; leave comfort root-room; let joy size
At God knows when to God knows what; whose smile
's not wrung, see you; unforeseen times rather—as
　　　　skies
Betweenpie mountains—lights a lovely mile.

THAT NATURE IS A HERACLITEAN FIRE AND OF THE COMFORT OF THE RESURRECTION

Cloud-puffball, torn tufts, tossed pillows |
　　flaunt forth, then chevy on an air-
built thoroughfare: heaven-roysterers, in gay-gangs |
　　they throng: they glitter in marches.
Down roughcast, down dazzling whitewash, | wher-
　　ever an elm arches,
Shivelights and shadowtackle in long | lashes lace, lance,
　　and pair.
Delightfully the bright wind boisterous | ropes,
　　wrestles, beats earth bare

59

Of yestertempest's creases; in pool and rut peel
parches
Squandering ooze to squeezed | dough, crust, dust;
stanches, starches
Squadroned masks and manmarks | treadmire toil there
Footfretted in it. Million-fuelèd, | nature's bonfire
burns on.
But quench her bonniest, dearest | to her, her clearest-
selvèd spark
Man, how fast his firedint, | his mark on mind, is gone!
Both are in an unfathomable, all is in an enormous dark
Drowned. O pity and indig | nation! Manshape, that
shone
Sheer off, disseveral, a star, | death blots black out;
nor mark
                    Is any of him at all so stark
But vastness blurs and time | beats level. Enough! the
Resurrection,
A heart's-clarion! Away grief's gasping, | joyless days,
dejection.
                    Across my foundering deck shone
A beacon, an eternal beam. | Flesh fade, and mortal
trash
Fall to the residuary worm; | world's wildfire, leave
but ash:
                    In a flash, at a trumpet crash,
I am all at once what Christ is, | since he was what I am,
and
This Jack, joke, poor potsherd, | patch, matchwood,
immortal diamond,
                    Is immortal diamond.

RED HANRAHAN'S SONG ABOUT IRELAND

The old brown thorn-trees break in two high over
    Cummen Strand,
Under a bitter black wind that blows from the left
    hand;
Our courage breaks like an old tree in a black wind
    and dies,
But we have hidden in our hearts the flame out of the
    eyes
Of Cathleen, the daughter of Houlihan.

The wind has bundled up the clouds high over Knock-
    narea,
And thrown the thunder on the stones for all that
    Maeve can say.
Angers that are like noisy clouds have set our hearts
    abeat;
But we have all bent low and low and kissed the quiet
    feet
Of Cathleen, the daughter of Houlihan.

The yellow pool has overflowed high up on Clooth-na-
    Bare,
For the wet winds are blowing out of the clinging air;
Like heavy flooded waters our bodies and our blood;
But purer than a tall candle before the Holy Rood
Is Cathleen, the daughter of Houlihan.

I know that I shall meet my fate
Somewhere among the clouds above;
Those that I fight I do not hate,
Those that I guard I do not love;
My country is Kiltartan Cross,
My countrymen Kiltartan's poor,
No likely end could bring them loss
Or leave them happier than before.
Nor law, nor duty bade me fight,
Nor public men, nor cheering crowds,
A lonely impulse of delight
Drove to this tumult in the clouds;
I balanced all, brought all to mind,
The years to come seemed waste of breath,
A waste of breath the years behind
In balance with this life, this death.

EASTER, 1916

I have met them at close of day
Coming with vivid faces
From counter or desk among grey
Eighteenth-century houses.
I have passed with a nod of the head
Or polite meaningless words,
Or have lingered awhile and said
Polite meaningless words,
And thought before I had done
Of a mocking tale or a gibe
To please a companion
Around the fire at the club,

Being certain that they and I
But lived where motley is worn:
All changed, changed utterly:
A terrible beauty is born.

That woman's days were spent
In ignorant good-will,
Her nights in argument
Until her voice grew shrill.
What voice more sweet than hers
When, young and beautiful,
She rode to harriers?
This man had kept a school
And rode our wingèd horse;
This other his helper and friend
Was coming into his force;
He might have won fame in the end,
So sensitive his nature seemed,
So daring and sweet his thought.
This other man I had dreamed
A drunken, vainglorious lout.
He had done most bitter wrong
To some who are near my heart,
Yet I number him in the song;
He, too, has resigned his part
In the casual comedy;
He, too, has been changed in his turn,
Transformed utterly:
A terrible beauty is born.

Hearts with one purpose alone
Through summer and winter seem
Enchanted to a stone
To trouble the living stream.

W. B.
YEATS

The horse that comes from the road,
The rider, the birds that range
From cloud to tumbling cloud,
Minute by minute they change;
A shadow of cloud on the stream
Changes minute by minute;
A horse-hoof slides on the brim,
And a horse plashes within it;
The long-legged moor-hens dive,
And hens to moor-cocks call;
Minute by minute they live:
The stone's in the midst of all.

Too long a sacrifice
Can make a stone of the heart.
O when may it suffice?
That is Heaven's part, our part
To murmur name upon name,
As a mother names her child
When sleep at last has come
On limbs that had run wild.
What is it but nightfall?
No, no, not night but death;
Was it needless death after all?
For England may keep faith
For all that is done and said.
We know their dream; enough
To know they dreamed and are dead;
And what if excess of love
Bewildered them till they died?
I write it out in a verse—
MacDonagh and MacBride
And Connolly and Pearse
Now and in time to be,

Wherever green is worn,
Are changed, changed utterly:
A terrible beauty is born.

W. B.
YEATS

September 25, 1916

THE SECOND COMING

Turning and turning in the widening gyre
The falcon cannot hear the falconer;
Things fall apart; the centre cannot hold;
Mere anarchy is loosed upon the world,
The blood-dimmed tide is loosed, and everywhere
The ceremony of innocence is drowned;
The best lack all conviction, while the worst
Are full of passionate intensity.

Surely some revelation is at hand;
Surely the Second Coming is at hand.
The Second Coming! Hardly are those words out
When a vast image out of *Spiritus Mundi*
Troubles my sight: somewhere in sands of the
    desert
A shape with lion body and the head of a man,
A gaze blank and pitiless as the sun,
Is moving its slow thighs, while all about it
Reel shadows of the indignant desert birds.
The darkness drops again; but now I know
That twenty centuries of stony sleep
Were vexed to nightmare by a rocking cradle,
And what rough beast, its hour come round at last,
Slouches towards Bethlehem to be born?

THE TOWER

I

What shall I do with this absurdity—
O heart, O troubled heart—this caricature,
Decrepit age that has been tied to me
As to a dog's tail?

           Never had I more
Excited, passionate, fantastical
Imagination, nor an ear and eye
That more expected the impossible—
No, not in boyhood when with rod and fly,
Or the humbler worm, I climbed Ben Bulben's back
And had the livelong summer day to spend.
It seems that I must bid the Muse go pack,
Choose Plato and Plotinus for a friend
Until imagination, ear and eye,
Can be content with argument and deal
In abstract things; or be derided by
A sort of battered kettle at the heel.

II

I pace upon the battlements and stare
On the foundations of a house, or where
Tree, like a sooty finger, starts from the earth;
And send imagination forth
Under the day's declining beam, and call
Images and memories
From ruin or from ancient trees,
For I would ask a question of them all.

Beyond that ridge lived Mrs. French, and once
When every silver candlestick or sconce
Lit up the dark mahogany and the wine,
A serving-man, that could divine

That most respected lady's every wish,
Ran and with the garden shears
Clipped an insolent farmer's ears
And brought them in a little covered dish.

Some few remembered still when I was young
A peasant girl commended by a song,
Who'd lived somewhere upon that rocky place,
And praised the colour of her face,
And had the greater joy in praising her,
Remembering that, if walked she there,
Farmers jostled at the fair
So great a glory did the song confer.

And certain men, being maddened by those rhymes,
Or else by toasting her a score of times,
Rose from the table and declared it right
To test their fancy by their sight;
But they mistook the brightness of the moon
For the prosaic light of day—
Music had driven their wits astray—
And one was drowned in the great bog of Cloone.

Strange, but the man who made the song was blind;
Yet, now I have considered it, I find
That nothing strange; the tragedy began
With Homer that was a blind man,
And Helen has all living hearts betrayed.
O may the moon and sunlight seem
One inextricable beam,
For if I triumph I must make men mad.

And I myself created Hanrahan
And drove him drunk or sober through the dawn
From somewhere in the neighbouring cottages.
Caught by an old man's juggleries

W. B.   He stumbled, tumbled, fumbled to and fro
YEATS   And had but broken knees for hire
        And horrible splendour of desire;
        I thought it all out twenty years ago:

        Good fellows shuffled cards in an old bawn;
        And when that ancient ruffian's turn was on
        He so bewitched the cards under his thumb
        That all but the one card became
        A pack of hounds and not a pack of cards,
        And that he changed into a hare.
        Hanrahan rose in frenzy there
        And followed up those baying creatures towards—

        O towards I have forgotten what—enough!
        I must recall a man that neither love
        Nor music nor an enemy's clipped ear
        Could, he was so harried, cheer;
        A figure that has grown so fabulous
        There's not a neighbour left to say
        When he finished his dog's day:
        An ancient bankrupt master of this house.

        Before that ruin came, for centuries,
        Rough men-at-arms, cross-gartered to the knees
        Or shod in iron, climbed the narrow stairs,
        And certain men-at-arms there were
        Whose images, in the Great Memory stored,
        Come with loud cry and panting breast
        To break upon a sleeper's rest
        While their great wooden dice beat on the board.

        As I would question all, come all who can;
        Come old, necessitous, half-mounted man;
        And bring beauty's blind rambling celebrant;
        The red man the juggler sent

Through God-forsaken meadows; Mrs. French,
Gifted with so fine an ear;
The man drowned in a bog's mire,
When mocking muses chose the country wench.

Did all old men and women, rich and poor,
Who trod upon these rocks or passed this door,
Whether in public or in secret rage
As I do now against old age?
But I have found an answer in those eyes
That are impatient to be gone;
Go therefore; but leave Hanrahan,
For I need all his mighty memories.

Old lecher with a love on every wind,
Bring up out of that deep considering mind
All that you have discovered in the grave,
For it is certain that you have
Reckoned up every unforeknown, unseeing
Plunge, lured by a softening eye,
Or by a touch or a sigh,
Into the labyrinth of another's being;

Does the imagination dwell the most
Upon a woman won or woman lost?
If on the lost, admit you turned aside
From a great labyrinth out of pride,
Cowardice, some silly over-subtle thought
Or anything called conscience once;
And that if memory recur, the sun's
Under eclipse and the day blotted out.

III

It is time that I wrote my will;
I choose upstanding men

69

That climb the streams until
The fountain leap, and at dawn
Drop their cast at the side
Of dripping stone; I declare
They shall inherit my pride,
The pride of people that were
Bound neither to Cause nor to State,
Neither to slaves that were spat on,
Nor to the tyrants that spat,
The people of Burke and of Grattan
That gave, though free to refuse—
Pride, like that of the morn,
When the headlong light is loose,
Or that of the fabulous horn,
Or that of the sudden shower
When all streams are dry,
Or that of the hour
When the swan must fix his eye
Upon a fading gleam,
Float out upon a long
Last reach of glittering stream
And there sing his last song.
And I declare my faith:
I mock Plotinus' thought
And cry in Plato's teeth,
Death and life were not
Till man made up the whole,
Made lock, stock and barrel
Out of his bitter soul,
Aye, sun and moon and star, all,
And further add to that
That, being dead, we rise,
Dream and so create
Translunar Paradise.

I have prepared my peace
With learned Italian things
And the proud stones of Greece,
Poet's imaginings
And memories of love,
Memories of the words of women,
All those things whereof
Man makes a superhuman
Mirror-resembling dream.

As at the loophole there
The daws chatter and scream,
And drop twigs layer upon layer.
When they have mounted up,
The mother bird will rest
On their hollow top,
And so warm her wild nest.

I leave both faith and pride
To young upstanding men
Climbing the mountain side,
That under bursting dawn
They may drop a fly;
Being of that metal made
Till it was broken by
This sedentary trade.

Now shall I make my soul,
Compelling it to study
In a learned school
Till the wreck of body,
Slow decay of blood,
Testy delirium
Or dull decrepitude,
Or what worse evil come—

W. B.   The death of friends, or death
Yeats   Of every brilliant eye
         That made a catch in the breath—
         Seem but the clouds of the sky
         When the horizon fades;
         Or a bird's sleepy cry
         Among the deepening shades.

1926

A DIALOGUE OF SELF AND SOUL

I

MY SOUL. I summon to the winding ancient stair;
    Set all your mind upon the steep ascent,
    Upon the broken, crumbling battlement,
    Upon the breathless starlit air,
    Upon the star that marks the hidden pole;
    Fix every wandering thought upon
    That quarter where all thought is done:
    Who can distinguish darkness from the soul?

MY SELF. The consecrated blade upon my knees
    Is Sato's ancient blade, still as it was,
    Still razor-keen, still like a looking-glass
    Unspotted by the centuries;
    That flowering, silken, old embroidery, torn
    From some court-lady's dress and round
    The wooden scabbard bound and wound,
    Can, tattered, still protect, faded adorn.

MY SOUL. Why should the imagination of a man
    Long past his prime remember things that are
    Emblematical of love and war?
    Think of ancestral night that can,

        If but imagination scorn the earth
        And intellect its wandering
        To this and that and t'other thing,
        Deliver from the crime of death and birth.

MY SELF. Montashigi, third of his family, fashioned it
        Five hundred years ago, about it lie
        Flowers from I know not what embroidery—
        Heart's purple—and all these I set
        For emblems of the day against the tower
        Emblematical of the night,
        And claim as by a soldier's right
        A charter to commit the crime once more.

MY SOUL. Such fullness in that quarter overflows
        And falls into the basin of the mind
        That man is stricken deaf and dumb and blind,
        For intellect no longer knows
        Is from the *Ought*, or *Knower* from the *Known*—
        That is to say, ascends to Heaven;
        Only the dead can be forgiven;
        But when I think of that my tongue's a stone.

II

MY SELF. A living man is blind and drinks his drop.
        What matter if the ditches are impure?
        What matter if I live it all once more?
        Endure that toil of growing up;
        The ignominy of boyhood; the distress
        Of boyhood changing into man;
        The unfinished man and his pain
        Brought face to face with his own clumsiness;

        The finished man among his enemies?—
        How in the name of Heaven can he escape

        73

That defiling and disfigured shape
The mirror of malicious eyes
Casts upon his eyes until at last
He thinks that shape must be his shape?
And what's the good of an escape
If honour find him in the wintry blast?

I am content to live it all again
And yet again, if it be life to pitch
Into the frog-spawn of a blind man's ditch,
A blind man battering blind men;
Or into that most fecund ditch of all,
The folly that man does
Or must suffer, if he woos
A proud woman not kindred of his soul.

I am content to follow to its source,
Every event in action or in thought;
Measure the lot; forgive myself the lot!
When such as I cast out remorse
So great a sweetness flows into the breast
We must laugh and we must sing,
We are blest by everything,
Everything we look upon is blest.

FOR ANNE GREGORY

'Never shall a young man,
Thrown into despair
By those great honey-coloured
Ramparts at your ear,
Love you for yourself alone
And not your yellow hair.'

74

'But I can get a hair-dye
And set such colour there,
Brown, or black, or carrot,
That young men in despair
May love me for myself alone
And not my yellow hair.'

'I heard an old religious man
But yesternight declare
That he had found a text to prove
That only God, my dear,
Could love you for yourself alone
And not your yellow hair.'

BYZANTIUM

The unpurged images of day recede;
The Emperor's drunken soldiery are abed;
Night resonance recedes, night-walkers' song
After great cathedral gong;
A starlit or a moonlit dome disdains
All that man is,
All mere complexities,
The fury and the mire of human veins.

Before me floats an image, man or shade,
Shade more than man, more image than a shade;
For Hades' bobbin bound in mummy-cloth
May unwind the winding path;
A mouth that has no moisture and no breath
Breathless mouths may summon;
I hail the superhuman;
I call it death-in-life and life-in-death.

W. B.
Yeats

Miracle, bird or golden handiwork,
More miracle than bird or handiwork,
Planted on the star-lit golden bough,
Can like the cocks of Hades crow,
Or, by the moon embittered, scorn aloud
In glory of changeless metal
Common bird or petal
And all complexities of mire or blood.

At midnight on the Emperor's pavement flit
Flames that no faggot feeds, nor steel has lit,
Nor storm disturbs, flames begotten of flame,
Where blood-begotten spirits come
And all complexities of fury leave,
Dying into a dance,
An agony of trance,
An agony of flame that cannot singe a sleeve.

Astraddle on the dolphin's mire and blood,
Spirit after spirit! The smithies break the flood,
The golden smithies of the Emperor!
Marbles of the dancing floor
Break bitter furies of complexity,
Those images that yet
Fresh images beget,
That dolphin-torn, that gong-tormented sea.

1930

T. E. HULME

AUTUMN

A touch of cold in the Autumn night—
I walked abroad,
And saw the ruddy moon lean over a hedge
Like a red-faced farmer.
I did not stop to speak, but nodded,
And round about were the wistful stars
With white faces like town children.

MANA ABODA

Beauty is the marking-time, the stationary vibration, the feigned ecstasy of an arrested impulse unable to reach its natural end.

Mana Aboda, whose bent form
The sky in archèd circle is,
Seems ever for an unknown grief to mourn.
Yet on a day I heard her cry:
'I weary of the roses and the singing poets—
Josephs all, not tall enough to try'.

ABOVE THE DOCK

Above the quiet dock in midnight,
Tangled in the tall mast's corded height,
Hangs the moon. What seemed so far away
Is but a child's balloon, forgotten after play.

THE EMBANKMENT

(The fantasia of a fallen gentleman on a cold, bitter night.)

Once, in finesse of fiddles found I ecstasy,
In a flash of gold heels on the hard pavement.
Now see I
That warmth's the very stuff of poesy.
Oh, God, make small
The old star-eaten blanket of the sky,
That I may fold it round me and in comfort lie.

CONVERSION

Light-hearted I walked into the valley wood
In the time of hyacinths,
Till beauty like a scented cloth
Cast over, stifled me. I was bound
Motionless and faint of breath
By loveliness that is her own eunuch.

Now pass I to the final river
Ignominiously, in a sack, without sound,
As any peeping Turk to the Bosphorus.

EZRA POUND

NEAR PERIGORD

*A Perigord, pres del muralh
       Tan que i puosch' om gitar ab malh.*

You'd have men's hearts up from the dust
And tell their secrets, Messire Cino,
Right enough? Then read between the lines of Uc St.
    Circ,
Solve me the riddle, for you know the tale.

Bertrans, En Bertrans, left a fine canzone:
'Maent, I love you, you have turned me out.
The voice at Montfort, Lady Agnes' hair,
Bel Miral's stature, the viscountess' throat,
Set all together, are not worthy of you . . .'
And all the while you sing out that canzone,
Think you that Maent lived at Montaignac,
One at Chalais, another at Malemort
Hard over Brive—for every lady a castle,
Each place strong.

               Oh, *is* it easy enough?
Tairiran held hall in Montaignac,
His brother-in-law was all there was of power
In Perigord, and this good union
Gobbled all the land, and held it later for some hun-
    dred years.
And our En Bertrans was in Altafort,
Hub of the wheel, the stirrer-up of strife,
As caught by Dante in the last wallow of hell—
The headless trunk 'that made its head a lamp',

79

For separation wrought out separation,
And he who set the strife between brother and brother
And had his way with the old English king,
Viced in such torture for the 'counterpass'.
How would you live, with neighbours set about you—
Poictiers and Brive, untaken Rochecouart,
Spread like the finger-tips of one frail hand;
And you on that great mountain of a palm—
Not a neat ledge, not Foix between its streams,
But one huge back half-covered up with pine,
Worked for and snatched from the string-purse of
      Born—
The four round towers, four brothers—mostly fools:
What could he do but play the desperate chess,
And stir old grudges?
          'Pawn your castles, lords!
Let the Jews pay.'
          And the great scene—
(That, maybe, never happened!)
          Beaten at last,
Before the hard old king:
          'Your son, ah, since he died
My wit and worth are cobwebs brushed aside
In the full flare of grief. Do what you will.'

    Take the whole man, and ravel out the story.
He loved this lady in castle Montaignac?
The castle flanked him—he had need of it.
You read to-day, how long the overlords of Perigord,
The Talleyrands, have held the place; it was no transient
    fiction.
And Maent failed him? Or saw through the scheme?

    And all his net-like thought of new alliance?
Chalais is high, a-level with the poplars.

Its lowest stones just meet the valley tips
Where the low Dronne is filled with water-lilies.
And Rochecouart can match it, stronger yet,
The very spur's end, built on sheerest cliff,
And Malemort keeps its close hold on Brive,
While Born, his own close purse, his rabbit warren,
His subterranean chamber with a dozen doors,
A-bristle with antennae to feel roads,
To sniff the traffic into Perigord.
And that hard phalanx, that unbroken line,
The ten good miles from there to Maent's castle,
All of his flank—how could he do without her?
And all the road to Cahors, to Toulouse?
What would he do without her?

 'Papiol,
Go forthright singing—Anhes, Cembelins.
There is a throat; ah, there are two white hands;
There is a trellis full of early roses,
And all my heart is bound about with love.
Where am I come with compound flatteries—
What doors are open to fine compliment?'
And every one half jealous of Maent?
He wrote the catch to pit their jealousies
Against her; give her pride in them?

Take his own speech, make what you will of it—
And still the knot, the first knot, of Maent?

 Is it a love poem? Did he sing of war?
Is it an intrigue to run subtly out,
Born of a jongleur's tongue, freely to pass
Up and about and in and out the land,
Mark him a craftsman and a strategist?
(St. Leider had done as much at Polhonac,

Ezra Singing a different stave, as closely hidden.)
Pound Oh, there is precedent, legal tradition,
To sing one thing when your song means another,
'Et albirar ab lor bordon—'
Foix' count knew that. What is Sir Bertrans' singing?
Maent, Maent, and yet again Maent,
Or war and broken heaumes and politics?

II

End fact. Try fiction. Let us say we see
En Bertrans, a tower-room at Hautefort,
Sunset, the ribbon-like road lies, in red cross-light,
Southward toward Montaignac, and he bends at a table
Scribbling, swearing between his teeth; by his left
hand
Lie little strips of parchment covered over,
Scratched and erased with al and ochaisos.
Testing his list of rhymes, a lean man? Bilious?
With a red straggling beard?
And the green cat's-eye lifts toward Montaignac.

Or take his 'magnet' singer setting out,
Dodging his way past Aubeterre, singing at Chalais
In the vaulted hall,
Or, by a lichened tree at Rochecouart
Aimlessly watching a hawk above the valleys,
Waiting his turn in the midsummer evening,
Thinking of Aelis, whom he loved heart and soul . . .
To find her half alone, Montfort away,
And a brown, placid, hated woman visiting her,
Spoiling his visit, with a year before the next one.
Little enough?
Or carry him forward. 'Go through all the courts,
My Magnet,' Bertrans had said.

We came to Ventadour
In the mid love court, he sings out the canzon,
No one hears save Arrimon Luc D'Esparo—
No one hears aught save the gracious sound of compli-
    ments.
Sir Arrimon counts on his fingers, Montfort,
Rochecouart, Chalais, the rest, the tactic,
Malemort, guesses beneath, sends word to Cœur-de-
    Lion:
The compact, de Born smoked out, trees felled
About his castle, cattle driven out!
Or no one sees it, and En Bertrans prospered?

And ten years after, or twenty, as you will,
Arnaut and Richard lodge beneath Chalus:
The dull round towers encroaching on the field,
The tents tight drawn, horses at tether
Farther and out of reach, the purple night,
The crackling of small fires, the bannerets,
The lazy leopards on the largest banner,
Stray gleams on hanging mail, an armourer's torch-flare
Melting on steel.

And in the quietest space
They probe old scandals, say de Born is dead;
And we've the gossip (skipped six hundred years).
Richard shall die to-morrow—leave him there
Talking of *trobar clus* with Daniel.
And the 'best craftsman' sings out his friend's song,
Envies its vigour . . . and deplores the technique,
Dispraises his own skill?—That's as you will.
And they discuss the dead man,
Plantagenet puts the riddle: 'Did he love her?'
And Arnaut parries: 'Did he love your sister?

EZRA True, he has praised her, but in some opinion
POUND He wrote that praise only to show he had
The favour of your party; had been well received.'
'You knew the man.'
'*You* knew the man.'
'I am an artist, you have tried both métiers.'
'You were born near him.'
'Do we know our friends?'
'Say that he saw the castles, say that he loved Maent!'
'Say that he loved her, does it solve the riddle?'
End the discussion, Richard goes out next day
And gets a quarrel-bolt shot through his vizard,
Pardons the bowman, dies,

Ends our discussion. Arnaut ends
'In sacred odour'—(that's apocryphal!)
And we can leave the talk till Dante writes:
Surely I saw, and still before my eyes
Goes on that headless trunk, that bears for light
Its own head swinging, gripped by the dead hair,
And like a swinging lamp that says, 'Ah me!
I severed men, my head and heart
Ye see here severed, my life's counterpart.'

Or take En Bertrans?

III

Ed eran due in uno, ed uno in due;
Inferno, XXVIII, 125

Bewildering spring, and by the Auvezere
Poppies and day's eyes in the green émail
Rose over us; and we knew all that stream,
And our two horses had traced out the valleys;

84

Knew the low flooded lands squared out with poplars,
In the young days when the deep sky befriended.   POUND
  And great wings beat above us in the twilight,
And the great wheels in heaven
Bore us together . . . surging . . . and apart . . .
Believing we should meet with lips and hands,
  High, high and sure . . . and then the counter-thrust:
'Why do you love me? Will you always love me?
But I am like the grass, I cannot love you.'
Or, 'Love, and I love and love you,
And hate your mind, not *you*, your soul, your hands.'

  So to this last estrangement, Tairiran!

  There shut up in his castle, Tairiran's,
She who had nor ears nor tongue save in her hands,
Gone—ah, gone—untouched, unreachable!
She who could never live save through one person,
She who could never speak save to one person,
And all the rest of her a shifting change,
A broken bundle of mirrors . . . !

EXILE'S LETTER

To So-Kin of Rakuyo, ancient friend, Chancellor of
    Gen.
Now I remember that you built me a special tavern
By the south side of the bridge at Ten-Shin.
With yellow gold and white jewels, we paid for songs
    and laughter
And we were drunk for month on month, forgetting
    the kings and princes.

Intelligent men came drifting in from the sea and from
the west border,
And with them, and with you especially
There was nothing at cross purpose,
And they made nothing of sea-crossing or of mountain-
crossing,
If only they could be of that fellowship,
And we all spoke out our hearts and minds, and with-
out regret.
And then I was sent off to South Wei,
smothered in laurel groves,
And you to the north of Raku-hoku
Till we had nothing but thoughts and memories in
common.

And then, when separation had come to its worst,
We met, and travelled into Sen-Go,
Through all the thirty-six folds of the turning and
twisting waters,
Into a valley of the thousand bright flowers,
That was the first valley;
And into ten thousand valleys full of voices and pine-
winds.
And with silver harness and reins of gold,
Out came the East of Kan foreman and his company.
And there came also the 'True man' of Shi-yo to meet
me,
Playing on a jewelled mouth-organ.
In the storied houses of San-Ko they gave us more
Sennin music,
Many instruments, like the sound of young phoenix
broods.
The foreman of Kan Chu, drunk, danced
because his long sleeves wouldn't keep still

With that music playing,
And I, wrapped in brocade, went to sleep with my head
    on his lap,
And my spirit so high it was all over the heavens,
And before the end of the day we were scattered like
    stars, or rain.
I had to be off to So, far away over the waters,
You back to your river-bridge.

And your father, who was brave as a leopard,
Was governor in Hei Shu, and put down the barbarian
    rabble.
And one May he had you send for me,
        despite the long distance.
And what with broken wheels and so on, I won't say it
    wasn't hard going,
Over roads twisted like sheep's guts.
And I was still going, late in the year,
        in the cutting wind from the North,
And thinking how little you cared for the cost,
        and you caring enough to pay it.
And what a reception:
Red jade cups, food well set on a blue jewelled table,
And I was drunk, and had no thought of returning.
And you would walk out with me to the western
    corner of the castle,
To the dynastic temple, with water about it clear as
    blue jade,
With boats floating, and the sound of mouth-organs
    and drums,
With ripples like dragon-scales, going grass-green on
    the water,
Pleasure lasting, with courtesans, going and coming
    without hindrance,

EZRA With the willow flakes falling like snow,
POUND And the vermilioned girls getting drunk about sunset,
And the water, a hundred feet deep, reflecting green
    eyebrows
—Eyebrows painted green are a fine sight in young
    moonlight,
Gracefully painted—
And the girls singing back at each other,
Dancing in transparent brocade,
And the wind lifting the song, and interrupting it,
Tossing it up under the clouds.

> And all this comes to an end.
> And is not again to be met with.

I went up to the court for examination,
Tried Layu's luck, offered the Choyo song,
And got no promotion,

> and went back to the East Mountains
> White-headed.

And once again, later, we met at the South bridge-head.
And then the crowd broke up, you went north to San
    palace,
And if you ask how I regret that parting:
It is like the flowers falling at Spring's end

> Confused, whirled in a tangle.

What is the use of talking, and there is no end of talk-
    ing,
There is no end of things in the heart.
I call in the boy,
Have him sit on his knees here

> To seal this,

And send it a thousand miles, thinking.

By Rihaku

POUR L'ELECTION DE SON SEPULCHRE

Ezra Pound

I

For three years, out of key with his time,
He strove to resuscitate the dead art
Of poetry; to maintain 'the sublime'
In the old sense. Wrong from the start—

No, hardly, but seeing he had been born
In a half-savage country, out of date;
Bent resolutely on wringing lilies from the acorn;
Capaneus; trout for factitious bait;

Ἴδμεν γάρ τοι πάνθ᾽, ὅσ᾽ ἐνὶ Τροίῃ
Caught in the unstopped ear;
Giving the rocks small lee-way
The chopped seas held him, therefore, that year.

His true Penelope was Flaubert,
He fished by obstinate isles;
Observed the elegance of Circe's hair
Rather than the mottoes on sundials.

Unaffected by 'the march of events',
He passed from men's memory in l'an trentiesme,
De son eage; the case presents
No adjunct to the Muses' diadem.

II

The age demanded an image
Of its accelerated grimace,
Something for the modern stage,
Not, at any rate, an Attic grace;

Not, not certainly, the obscure reveries
Of the inward gaze;

Better mendacities
Than the classics in paraphrase!

The 'age demanded' chiefly a mould in plaster,
Made with no loss of time,
A prose kinema, not, not assuredly, alabaster
Or the 'sculpture' of rhyme.

III

The tea-rose tea-gown, etc.
Supplants the mousseline of Cos,
The pianola 'replaces'
Sappho's barbitos.

Christ follows Dionysus,
Phallic and ambrosial
Made way for macerations;
Caliban casts out Ariel.

All things are a flowing,
Sage Heracleitus says;
But a tawdry cheapness
Shall outlast our days.

Even the Christian beauty
Defects—after Samothrace;
We see τὸ καλὸν
Decreed in the market-place.

Faun's flesh is not to us,
Nor the saint's vision.
We have the Press for wafer;
Franchise for circumcision.

All men, in law, are equals.
Free of Pisistratus,
We choose a knave or an eunuch
To rule over us.

O bright Apollo,
τίν' ἄνδρα, τίν' ἥρωα, τίνα θεὸν
What god, man, or hero
Shall I place a tin wreath upon!

IV

These fought in any case,
and some believing,
                    pro domo, in any case . . .

Some quick to arm,
some for adventure,
some from fear of weakness,
some from fear of censure,
some for love of slaughter, in imagination,
learning later . . .
some in fear, learning love of slaughter;

Died some, pro patria,
        non 'dulce' non 'et decor' . . .
walked eye-deep in hell
believing in old men's lies, then unbelieving
came home, home to a lie,
home to many deceits,
home to old lies and new infamy;
usury age-old and age-thick
and liars in public places.

Daring as never before, wastage as never before.
Young blood and high blood,
fair cheeks, and fine bodies;

fortitude as never before

frankness as never before,
disillusions as never told in the old days,
hysterias, trench confessions,
laughter out of dead bellies.

V

There died a myriad,
And of the best, among them,
For an old bitch gone in the teeth,
For a botched civilization,

Charm, smiling at the good mouth,
Quick eyes gone under earth's lid,

For two gross of broken statues,
For a few thousand battered books.

HOMAGE TO SEXTUS PROPERTIUS: XII

Who, who will be the next man to entrust his girl to
    a friend?
             Love interferes with fidelities;
The gods have brought shame on their relatives;
             Each man wants the pomegranate for himself;
Amiable and harmonious people are pushed incontinent
    into duels,
A Trojan and adulterous person came to Menelaus
    under the rites of hospitium,
And there was a case in Colchis, Jason and that woman
    in Colchis;
And besides, Lynceus,
             you were drunk.

Could you endure such promiscuity?
             She was not renowned for fidelity;
But to jab a knife in my vitals, to have passed on a swig
    of poison,
Preferable, my dear boy, my dear Lynceus,

Comrade, comrade of my life, of my purse, of my
        person;
But in one bed, in one bed alone, my dear Lynceus,
            I deprecate your attendance;
I would ask a like boon of Jove.

And you write of Acheloüs, who contended with
        Hercules;
You write of Adrastus' horses and the funeral rites of
        Achenor,
And you will not leave off imitating Aeschylus.
            Though you make a hash of Antimachus,
You think you are going to do Homer.
            And still a girl scorns the gods,
Of all these young women
            not one has enquired the cause of the world,
Nor the modus of lunar eclipses
            Nor whether there be any patch left of us
After we cross the infernal ripples,
            nor if the thunder fall from predestination;
Nor anything else of importance.

Upon the Actian marshes Virgil is Phoebus' chief of
        police,
            He can tabulate Caesar's great ships.
He thrills to Ilian arms,
            He shakes the Trojan weapons of Aeneas,
And casts stores on Lavinian beaches.
Make way, ye Roman authors,
                    clear the street O ye Greeks,
For a much larger Iliad is in the course of construction
                        (and to Imperial order)
Clear the streets O ye Greeks!

93

And you also follow him 'neath Phrygian pine shade':
Thyrsis and Daphnis upon whittled reeds,
And how ten sins can corrupt young maidens;
Kids for a bribe and pressed udders,
Happy selling poor loves for cheap apples.

Tityrus might have sung the same vixen;
Corydon tempted Alexis,
Head farmers do likewise, and lying weary amid their
oats
They get praise from tolerant Hamadryads.

Go on, to Ascraeus' prescription, the ancient,
respected, Wordsworthian:
'A flat field for rushes, grapes grow on the slope.'

And behold me, a small fortune left in my house.
Me, who had no general for a grandfather!
I shall triumph among young ladies of indeterminate
character,
My talent acclaimed in their banquets,
I shall be honoured with yesterday's wreaths.

And the god strikes to the marrow.

Like a trained and performing tortoise,
I would make verse in your fashion, if she should com-
mand it,
With her husband asking a remission of sentence,
And even this infamy would not attract
numerous readers
Were there an erudite or violent passion,
For the nobleness of the populace brooks nothing
below its own altitude.

94

One must have resonance, resonance and sonority . . . EZRA
like a goose. POUND

Varro sang Jason's expedition,
        Varro, of his great passion Leucadia,
There is song in the parchment; Catullus the highly
    indecorous,
Of Lesbia, known above Helen;
And in the dyed pages of Calvus,
        Calvus mourning Quintilia,
And but now Gallus had sung of Lycoris.
        Fair, fairest Lycoris—
The waters of Styx poured over the wound:
And now Propertius of Cynthia, taking his stand
    among these.

CANTO XIII

Kung walked
        by the dynastic temple
and into the cedar grove,
        and then out by the lower river,
And with him Khieu Tchi
        and Tian the low speaking
And 'we are unknown', said Kung,
You will take up charioteering?
        'Then you will become known,
'Or perhaps I should take up charioteering, or archery?
'Or the practice of public speaking?'
And Tseu-lou said, 'I would put the defences in order,'
And Khieu said, 'If I were lord of a province
I would put it in better order than this is.'
And Tchi said, 'I should prefer a small mountain
    temple,

'With order in the observances,
             with a suitable performance of the ritual,'
And Tian said, with his hand on the strings of his lute
The low sounds continuing
             after his hand left the strings,
And the sound went up like smoke, under the leaves,
And he looked after the sound:
             'The old swimming hole,
'And the boys flopping off the planks,
'Or sitting in the underbrush playing mandolins.'
             And Kung smiled upon all of them equally.
And Thseng-sie desired to know:
             'Which had answered correctly?'
And Kung said, 'They have all answered correctly,
'That is to say, each in his nature.'
And Kung raised his cane against Yuan Jang,
             Yuan Jang being his elder,
For Yuan Jang sat by the roadside pretending to
             be receiving wisdom.
And Kung said
             'You old fool, come out of it,
'Get up and do something useful.'
             And Kung said
'Respect a child's faculties
'From the moment it inhales the clear air,
'But a man of fifty who knows nothing
             'Is worthy of no respect.'
And 'When the prince has gathered about him
'All the savants and artists, his riches will be fully
             employed.'
And Kung said, and wrote on the bo leaves:
             'If a man have not order within him
'He can not spread order about him;
'And if a man have not order within him

96

'His family will not act with due order;
         'And if the prince have not order within him
'He can not put order in his dominions.'
And Kung gave the words 'order'
and 'brotherly deference'
And said nothing of the 'life after death'.
And he said
         'Anyone can run to excesses,
'It is easy to shoot past the mark,
'It is hard to stand firm in the middle.'

And they said: 'If a man commit murder
         'Should his father protect him, and hide him?'
And Kung said:
         'He should hide him.'

And Kung gave his daughter to Kong-Tchang
         Although Kong-Tchang was in prison.
And he gave his niece to Nan-Young
         although Nan-Young was out of office.
And Kung said 'Wang ruled with moderation,
         'In his day the State was well kept,
'And even I can remember
'A day when the historians left blanks in their writings,
'I mean for things they didn't know,
'But that time seems to be passing.'
And Kung said, 'Without character you will
         be unable to play on that instrument
'Or to execute the music fit for the Odes.
'The blossoms of the apricot
         blow from the east to the west,
'And I have tried to keep them from falling.'

SWEENEY AMONG THE NIGHTINGALES

ὤμοι, πέπληγμαι καιρίαν πληγὴν ἔσω.

Apeneck Sweeney spreads his knees
Letting his arms hang down to laugh,
The zebra stripes along his jaw
Swelling to maculate giraffe.

The circles of the stormy moon
Slide westward toward the River Plate,
Death and the Raven drift above
And Sweeney guards the horned gate.

Gloomy Orion and the Dog
Are veiled; and hushed the shrunken seas;
The person in the Spanish cape
Tries to sit on Sweeney's knees

Slips and pulls the table cloth
Overturns a coffee-cup,
Reorganised upon the floor
She yawns and draws a stocking up;

The silent man in mocha brown
Sprawls at the window-sill and gapes;
The waiter brings in oranges
Bananas figs and hothouse grapes;

The silent vertebrate in brown
Contracts and concentrates, withdraws;
Rachel *née* Rabinovitch
Tears at the grapes with murderous paws;

She and the lady in the cape
Are suspect, thought to be in league;
Therefore the man with heavy eyes
Declines the gambit, shows fatigue,

Leaves the room and reappears
Outside the window, leaning in,
Branches of wistaria
Circumscribe a golden grin;

The host with someone indistinct
Converses at the door apart,
The nightingales are singing near
The Convent of the Sacred Heart,

And sang within the bloody wood
When Agamemnon cried aloud,
And let their liquid siftings fall
To stain the stiff dishonoured shroud.

THE WASTE LAND

'*NAM Sibyllam quidem Cumis ego ipse oculis
meis vidi in ampulla pendere, et cum illi pueri
dicerent:* Σιβυλλα τί θέλεις; *respondebat illa:*
ἀποθανεῖν θέλω.'

For Ezra Pound
il miglior fabbro

I. THE BURIAL OF THE DEAD

April is the cruellest month, breeding
Lilacs out of the dead land, mixing
Memory and desire, stirring
Dull roots with spring rain.
Winter kept us warm, covering
Earth in forgetful snow, feeding
A little life with dried tubers.
Summer surprised us, coming over the Starnbergersee
With a shower of rain; we stopped in the colonnade,
And went on in sunlight, into the Hofgarten,   10
And drank coffee, and talked for an hour.
Bin gar keine Russin, stamm' aus Litauen, echt deutsch.
And when we were children, staying at the archduke's,
My cousin's, he took me out on a sled,
And I was frightened. He said, Marie,
Marie, hold on tight. And down we went.
In the mountains, there you feel free.
I read, much of the night, and go south in the winter.

What are the roots that clutch, what branches grow
Out of this stony rubbish? Son of man,   20
You cannot say, or guess, for you know only
A heap of broken images, where the sun beats,
And the dead tree gives no shelter, the cricket no
      relief,

And the dry stone no sound of water. Only
There is shadow under this red rock,
(Come in under the shadow of this red rock),
And I will show you something different from either
Your shadow at morning striding behind you
Or your shadow at evening rising to meet you;
I will show you fear in a handful of dust.   30

> *Frisch weht der Wind*
> *Der Heimat zu,*
> *Mein Irisch Kind,*
> *Wo weilest du?*

'You gave me hyacinths first a year ago;
'They called me the hyacinth girl.'
—Yet when we came back, late, from the Hyacinth
    garden,
Your arms full, and your hair wet, I could not
Speak, and my eyes failed, I was neither
Living nor dead, and I knew nothing,   40
Looking into the heart of light, the silence.
Od' und leer das Meer.

Madame Sosostris, famous clairvoyante,
Had a bad cold, nevertheless
Is known to be the wisest woman in Europe,
With a wicked pack of cards. Here, said she,
Is your card, the drowned Phoenician Sailor,
(Those are pearls that were his eyes. Look!)
Here is Belladonna, the Lady of the Rocks,
The lady of situations.   50
Here is the man with three staves, and here the Wheel,
And here is the one-eyed merchant, and this card,
Which is blank, is something he carries on his back,

Which I am forbidden to see. I do not find
The Hanged Man. Fear death by water.
I see crowds of people, walking round in a ring.
Thank you. If you see dear Mrs. Equitone,
Tell her I bring the horoscope myself:
One must be so careful these days.

Unreal City,   60
Under the brown fog of a winter dawn,
A crowd flowed over London Bridge, so many,
I had not thought death had undone so many.
Sighs, short and infrequent, were exhaled,
And each man fixed his eyes before his feet.
Flowed up the hill and down King William Street,
To where Saint Mary Woolnoth kept the hours
With a dead sound on the final stroke of nine.
There I saw one I knew, and stopped him, crying:
      'Stetson!
'You who were with me in the ships at Mylae!   70
'That corpse you planted last year in your garden,
'Has it begun to sprout? Will it bloom this year?
'Or has the sudden frost disturbed its bed?
'Oh keep the Dog far hence, that's friend to men,
'Or with his nails he'll dig it up again!
'You! hypocrite lecteur!—mon semblable,—mon
      frère!'

II. A GAME OF CHESS

The Chair she sat in, like a burnished throne,
Glowed on the marble, where the glass
Held up by standards wrought with fruited vines
From which a golden Cupidon peeped out   80
(Another hid his eyes behind his wing)
Doubled the flames of sevenbranched candelabra

Reflecting light upon the table as
The glitter of her jewels rose to meet it,
From satin cases poured in rich profusion;
In vials of ivory and coloured glass
Unstoppered, lurked her strange synthetic perfumes,
Unguent, powdered, or liquid—troubled, confused
And drowned the sense in odours; stirred by the air
That freshened from the window, these ascended   90
In fattening the prolonged candle-flames,
Flung their smoke into the laquearia,
Stirring the pattern on the coffered ceiling.
Huge sea-wood fed with copper
Burned green and orange, framed by the coloured
          stone,
In which sad light a carvèd dolphin swam.
Above the antique mantel was displayed
As though a window gave upon the sylvan scene
The change of Philomel, by the barbarous king
So rudely forced; yet there the nightingale   100
Filled all the desert with inviolable voice
And still she cried, and still the world pursues,
'Jug Jug' to dirty ears.
And other withered stumps of time
Were told upon the walls; staring forms
Leaned out, leaning, hushing the room enclosed.
Footsteps shuffled on the stair.
Under the firelight, under the brush, her hair
Spread out in fiery points
Glowed into words, then would be savagely still.   110

'My nerves are bad to-night. Yes, bad. Stay with me.
'Speak to me. Why do you never speak. Speak.
    'What are you thinking of? What thinking? What?
'I never know what you are thinking. Think.'

T. S. I think we are in rats' alley
ELIOT Where the dead men lost their bones.

'What is that noise?'
                        The wind under the door.
'What is that noise now? What is the wind doing?'
                        Nothing again nothing.   120
                                    'Do
'You know nothing? Do you see nothing? Do you
    remember
'Nothing?'
        I remember
Those are pearls that were his eyes.
'Are you alive, or not? Is there nothing in your head?'
                                                    But

O O O O that Shakespeherian Rag—
It's so elegant
So intelligent   130
'What shall I do now? What shall I do?'
'I shall rush out as I am, and walk the street
'With my hair down, so. What shall we do tomorrow?
'What shall we ever do?'
                        The hot water at ten.
And if it rains, a closed car at four.
And we shall play a game of chess,
Pressing lidless eyes and waiting for a knock upon the
    door.

When Lil's husband got demobbed, I said—
I didn't mince my words, I said to her myself,   140
HURRY UP PLEASE ITS TIME
Now Albert's coming back, make yourself a bit smart.
He'll want to know what you done with that money he
    gave you

104

To get yourself some teeth. He did, I was there.

You have them all out, Lil, and get a nice set,
He said, I swear, I can't bear to look at you.
And no more can't I, I said, and think of poor Albert,
He's been in the army four years, he wants a good time,
And if you don't give it him, there's others will, I said.
Oh is there, she said. Something o' that, I said.   150
Then I'll know who to thank, she said, and give me a
      straight look.
HURRY UP PLEASE ITS TIME
If you don't like it you can get on with it, I said,
Others can pick and choose if you can't.
But if Albert makes off, it won't be for lack of telling.
You ought to be ashamed, I said, to look so antique.
(And her only thirty-one.)
I can't help it, she said, pulling a long face,
It's them pills I took, to bring it off, she said.
(She's had five already, and nearly died of young
      George.)   160
The chemist said it would be all right, but I've never
      been the same.
You *are* a proper fool, I said.
Well, if Albert won't leave you alone, there it is, I
      said,
What you get married for if you don't want children?
HURRY UP PLEASE ITS TIME
Well, that Sunday Albert was home, they had a hot
      gammon,
And they asked me in to dinner, to get the beauty of it
      hot—
HURRY UP PLEASE ITS TIME
HURRY UP PLEASE ITS TIME
Goonight Bill. Goonight Lou. Goonight May. Goo-
      night.   170

T. S. Ta ta. Goonight. Goonight.
Eliot Good night, ladies, good night, sweet ladies, good
          night, good night.

III. THE FIRE SERMON

The river's tent is broken: the last fingers of leaf
Clutch and sink into the wet bank. The wind
Crosses the brown land, unheard. The nymphs are
          departed.
Sweet Thames, run softly, till I end my song.
The river bears no empty bottles, sandwich papers,
Silk handkerchiefs, cardboard boxes, cigarette ends
Or other testimony of summer nights. The nymphs are
          departed.
And their friends, the loitering heirs of city direc-
          tors;   180
Departed, have left no addresses.
By the waters of Leman I sat down and wept . . .
Sweet Thames, run softly till I end my song,
Sweet Thames, run softly, for I speak not loud or long.
But at my back in a cold blast I hear
The rattle of the bones, and chuckle spread from ear to
          ear.
A rat crept softly through the vegetation
Dragging its slimy belly on the bank
While I was fishing in the dull canal
On a winter evening round behind the gashouse   190
Musing upon the king my brother's wreck
And on the king my father's death before him.
White bodies naked on the low damp ground
And bones cast in a little low dry garret,
Rattled by the rat's foot only, year to year.
But at my back from time to time I hear

106

The sound of horns and motors, which shall bring
Sweeney to Mrs. Porter in the spring.
O the moon shone bright on Mrs. Porter
And on her daughter   ·200
They wash their feet in soda water
Et O ces voix d'enfants, chantant dans la coupole!

Twit twit twit
Jug jug jug jug jug jug
So rudely forc'd.
Tereu
Unreal City
Under the brown fog of a winter noon
Mr. Eugenides, the Smyrna merchant
Unshaven, with a pocket full of currants   210
C.i.f. London: documents at sight,
Asked me in demotic French
To luncheon at the Cannon Street Hotel
Followed by a weekend at the Metropole.

At the violet hour, when the eyes and back
Turn upward from the desk, when the human engine
      waits
Like a taxi throbbing waiting,
I Tiresias, though blind, throbbing between two lives,
Old man with wrinkled female breasts, can see
At the violet hour, the evening hour that strives   220
Homeward, and brings the sailor home from sea,
The typist home at teatime, clears her breakfast, lights
Her stove, and lays out food in tins.
Out of the window perilously spread
Her drying combinations touched by the sun's last rays,
On the divan are piled (at night her bed)
Stockings, slippers, camisoles, and stays.

I Tiresias, old man with wrinkled dugs
Perceived the scene, and foretold the rest—
I too awaited the expected guest.   230
He, the young man carbuncular, arrives,
A small house agent's clerk, with one bold stare,
One of the low on whom assurance sits
As a silk hat on a Bradford millionaire.
The time is now propitious, as he guesses,
The meal is ended, she is bored and tired,
Endeavours to engage her in caresses
Which still are unreproved, if undesired.
Flushed and decided, he assaults at once;
Exploring hands encounter no defence;   240
His vanity requires no response,
And makes a welcome of indifference.
(And I Tiresias have foresuffered all
Enacted on this same divan or bed;
I who have sat by Thebes below the wall
And walked among the lowest of the dead.)
Bestows one final patronising kiss,
And gropes his way, finding the stairs unlit . . .

She turns and looks a moment in the glass,
Hardly aware of her departed lover;   250
Her brain allows one half-formed thought to pass:
'Well now that's done: and I'm glad it's over.'
When lovely woman stoops to folly and
Paces about her room again, alone,
She smoothes her hair with automatic hand,
And puts a record on the gramophone.

'This music crept by me upon the waters'
And along the Strand, up Queen Victoria Street.
O City city, I can sometimes hear

Beside a public bar in Lower Thames Street,
The pleasant whining of a mandoline
And a clatter and a chatter from within
Where fishmen lounge at noon: where the walls
Of Magnus Martyr hold
Inexplicable splendour of Ionian white and gold.

      The river sweats
      Oil and tar
      The barges drift
      With the turning tide
      Red sails   270
      Wide
      To leeward, swing on the heavy spar.
      The barges wash
      Drifting logs
      Down Greenwich reach
      Past the Isle of Dogs.
              Weialala leia
              Wallala leialala
      Elizabeth and Leicester
      Beating oars   280
      The stern was formed
      A gilded shell
      Red and gold
      The brisk swell
      Rippled both shores
      Southwest wind
      Carried down stream
      The peal of bells
      White towers
              Weialala leia   290
              Wallala leialala

'Trams and dusty trees.
Highbury bore me. Richmond and Kew
Undid me. By Richmond I raised my knees
Supine on the floor of a narrow canoe.'

'My feet are at Moorgate, and my heart
Under my feet. After the event
He wept. He promised "a new start."
I made no comment. What should I resent?'

'On Margate Sands.   300
I can connect
Nothing with nothing.
The broken fingernails of dirty hands.
My people humble people who expect
Nothing.'
          la la

To Carthage then I came

Burning burning burning burning
O Lord Thou pluckest me out
O Lord Thou pluckest   310

burning

IV. DEATH BY WATER

Phlebas the Phoenician, a fortnight dead,
Forgot the cry of gulls, and the deep sea swell
And the profit and loss.
               A current under sea
Picked his bones in whispers. As he rose and fell
He passed the stages of his age and youth
Entering the whirlpool.
              Gentile or Jew

O you who turn the wheel and look to windward,   320   T. S.
Consider Phlebas, who was once handsome and tall as   ELIOT
    you.

V. WHAT THE THUNDER SAID

After the torchlight red on sweaty faces
After the frosty silence in the gardens
After the agony in stony places
The shouting and the crying
Prison and palace and reverberation
Of thunder of spring over distant mountains
He who was living is now dead
We who were living are now dying
With a little patience   330

Here is no water but only rock
Rock and no water and the sandy road
The road winding above among the mountains
Which are mountains of rock without water
If there were water we should stop and drink
Amongst the rock one cannot stop or think
Sweat is dry and feet are in the sand
If there were only water amongst the rock
Dead mountain mouth of carious teeth that cannot spit
Here one can neither stand nor lie nor sit   340
There is not even silence in the mountains
But dry sterile thunder without rain
There is not even solitude in the mountains
But red sullen faces sneer and snarl
From doors of mudcracked houses
                                        If there were water
    And no rock
    If there were rock

III

And also water
And water   350
A spring
A pool among the rock
If there were the sound of water only
Not the cicada
And dry grass singing
But sound of water over a rock
Where the hermit-thrush sings in the pine trees
Drip drop drip drop drop drop drop
But there is no water

Who is the third who walks always beside you?
When I count, there are only you and I together   360
But when I look ahead up the white road
There is always another one walking beside you
Gliding wrapt in a brown mantle, hooded
I do not know whether a man or a woman
—But who is that on the other side of you?

What is that sound high in the air
Murmur of maternal lamentation
Who are those hooded hordes swarming
Over endless plains, stumbling in cracked earth
Ringed by the flat horizon only   370
What is the city over the mountains
Cracks and reforms and bursts in the violet air
Falling towers
Jerusalem Athens Alexandria
Vienna London
Unreal

A woman drew her long black hair out tight
And fiddled whisper music on those strings
And bats with baby faces in the violet light

Whistled, and beat their wings 380
And crawled head downward down a blackened wall
And upside down in air were towers
Tolling reminiscent bells, that kept the hours
And voices singing out of empty cisterns and exhausted
     wells.

In this decayed hole among the mountains
In the faint moonlight, the grass is singing
Over the tumbled graves, about the chapel
There is the empty chapel, only the wind's home.
It has no windows, and the door swings,
Dry bones can harm no one. 390
Only a cock stood on the rooftree
Co co rico co co rico
In a flash of lightning. Then a damp gust
Bringing rain

Ganga was sunken, and the limp leaves
Waited for rain, while the black clouds
Gathered far distant, over Himavant.
The jungle crouched, humped in silence.
Then spoke the thunder
DA 400
Datta : what have we given?
My friend, blood shaking my heart
The awful daring of a moment's surrender
Which an age of prudence can never retract
By this, and this only, we have existed
Which is not to be found in our obituaries
Or in memories draped by the beneficent spider
Or under seals broken by the lean solicitor
In our empty rooms
DA 410

T. S. *Dayadhvam* : I have heard the key
ELIOT Turn in the door once and turn once only
We think of the key, each in his prison
Thinking of the key, each confirms a prison
Only at nightfall, aethereal rumours
Revive for a moment a broken Coriolanus
DA
Damyata : The boat responded
Gaily, to the hand expert with sail and oar
The sea was calm, your heart would have responded 420
Gaily, when invited, beating obedient
To controlling hands

                                      I sat upon the shore
Fishing, with the arid plain behind me
Shall I at least set my lands in order?
London Bridge is falling down falling down falling
    down
Poi s'ascose nel foco che gli affina
Quando fiam ceu chelidon—O swallow swallow
Le Prince d'Aquitaine à la tour abolie
These fragments I have shored against my ruins   430
Why then Ile fit you. Hieronymo's mad againe.
Datta. Dayadhvam. Damyata.
             Shantih   shantih   shantih

JOURNEY OF THE MAGI

T. S.
ELIOT

'A cold coming we had of it,
Just the worst time of the year
For a journey, and such a long journey:
The ways deep and the weather sharp,
The very dead of winter.'
And the camels galled, sore-footed, refractory,
Lying down in the melting snow.
There were times we regretted
The summer palaces on slopes, the terraces,
And the silken girls bringing sherbet.
Then the camel men cursing and grumbling
And running away, and wanting their liquor and
    women,
And the night-fires going out, and the lack of shelters,
And the cities hostile and the towns unfriendly
And the villages dirty and charging high prices:
A hard time we had of it.
At the end we preferred to travel all night,
Sleeping in snatches,
With the voices singing in our ears, saying
That this was all folly.

Then at dawn we came down to a temperate valley,
Wet, below the snow line, smelling of vegetation;
With a running stream and a water-mill beating the
    darkness,
And three trees on the low sky,
And an old white horse galloped away in the meadow.
Then we came to a tavern with vine-leaves over the
    lintel,
Six hands at an open door dicing for pieces of silver,
And feet kicking the empty wine-skins.
But there was no information, and so we continued

And arrived at evening, not a moment too soon
Finding the place; it was (you may say) satisfactory.

All this was a long time ago, I remember,
And I would do it again, but set down
This set down
This: were we led all that way for
Birth or Death? There was a Birth, certainly,
We had evidence and no doubt. I had seen birth and
    death,
But had thought they were different; this Birth was
Hard and bitter agony for us, like Death, our death.
We returned to our places, these Kingdoms,
But no longer at ease here, in the old dispensation,
With an alien people clutching their gods.
I should be glad of another death.

From ASH WEDNESDAY

I

Because I do not hope to turn again
Because I do not hope
Because I do not hope to turn
Desiring this man's gift and that man's scope
I no longer strive to strive towards such things
(Why should the agèd eagle stretch its wings?)
Why should I mourn
The vanished power of the usual reign ?

Because I do not hope to know again
The infirm glory of the positive hour
Because I do not think
Because I know I shall not know
The one veritable transitory power

Because I cannot drink
There, where trees flower, and springs flow, for there
    is nothing again

Because I know that time is always time
And place is always and only place
And what is actual is actual only for one time
And only for one place
I rejoice that things are as they are and
I renounce the blessèd face
And renounce the voice
Because I cannot hope to turn again

Consequently I rejoice, having to construct some-
    thing
Upon which to rejoice

And pray to God to have mercy upon us
And I pray that I may forget
These matters that with myself I too much discuss
Too much explain
Because I do not hope to turn again
Let these words answer
For what is done, not to be done again
May the judgement not be too heavy upon us

Because these wings are no longer wings to fly
But merely vans to beat the air
The air which is now thoroughly small and dry
Smaller and dryer than the will
Teach us to care and not to care
Teach us to sit still.

Pray for us sinners now and at the hour of our death
Pray for us now and at the hour of our death.

Lady, three white leopards sat under a juniper-tree
In the cool of the day, having fed to satiety
On my legs my heart my liver and that which had been
    contained
In the hollow round of my skull. And God said
Shall these bones live? shall these
Bones live? And that which had been contained
In the bones (which were already dry) said chirping:
Because of the goodness of this Lady
And because of her loveliness, and because
She honours the Virgin in meditation,
We shine with brightness. And I who am here dis-
    sembled
Proffer my deeds to oblivion, and my love
To the posterity of the desert and the fruit of the
    gourd.
It is this which recovers
My guts the strings of my eyes and the indigestible
    portions
Which the leopards reject. The Lady is withdrawn
In a white gown, to contemplation, in a white gown.
Let the whiteness of bones atone to forgetfulness.
There is no life in them. As I am forgotten
And would be forgotten, so I would forget
Thus devoted, concentrated in purpose. And God said
Prophesy to the wind, to the wind only for only
The wind will listen. And the bones sang chirping
With the burden of the grasshopper, saying

Lady of silences
Calm and distressed
Torn and most whole
Rose of memory

Rose of forgetfulness
Exhausted and life-giving
Worried reposeful
The single Rose
Is now the Garden
Where all loves end
Terminate torment
Of love unsatisfied
The greater torment
Of love satisfied
End of the endless
Journey to no end
Conclusion of all that
Is inconclusible
Speech without word and
Word of no speech
Grace to the Mother
For the Garden
Where all love ends.

Under a juniper-tree the bones sang, scattered and
    shining
We are glad to be scattered, we did little good to each
    other,
Under a tree in the cool of the day, with the blessing
    of sand,
Forgetting themselves and each other, united
In the quiet of the desert. This is the land which ye
Shall divide by lot. And neither division nor unity
Matters. This is the land. We have our inheritance.

MARINA

Quis hic locus, quae regio, quae mundi plaga?

What seas what shores what grey rocks and what
  islands
What water lapping the bow
And scent of pine and the woodthrush singing through
  the fog
What images return
O my daughter.

Those who sharpen the tooth of the dog, meaning
Death
Those who glitter with the glory of the humming bird,
  meaning
Death
Those who sit in the stye of contentment, meaning
Death
Those who suffer the ecstasy of the animals, meaning
Death

Are become unsubstantial, reduced by a wind,
A breath of pine, and the woodsong fog
By this grace dissolved in place

What is this face less clear and clearer
The pulse in the arm, less strong and stronger—
Given or lent? more distant than stars and nearer than
  the eye
Whispers and small laughter between leaves and
  hurrying feet
Under sleep, where all the waters meet.

Bowsprit cracked with ice and paint cracked with heat.
I made this, I have forgotten

And remember.
The rigging weak and the canvas rotten
Between one June and another September.
Made this unknowing, half conscious, unknown, my
        own.
The garboard strake leaks, the seams need caulking.
This form, this face, this life
Living to live in a world of time beyond me; let me
Resign my life for this life, my speech for that un-
        spoken,
The awakened, lips parted, the hope, the new ships.

What seas what shores what granite islands towards
        my timbers
And woodthrush calling through the fog
My daughter.

TRIUMPHAL MARCH

Stone, bronze, stone, steel, stone, oakleaves, horses'
        heels
Over the paving.
And the flags. And the trumpets. And so many eagles.
How many? Count them. And such a press of people.
We hardly knew ourselves that day, or knew the City.
This is the way to the temple, and we so many crowd-
        ing the way.
So many waiting, how many waiting? what did it
        matter, on such a day?
Are they coming? No, not yet. You can see some eagles.
            And hear the trumpets.
Here they come. Is he coming?
The natural wakeful life of our Ego is a perceiving.

T. S. We can wait with our stools and our sausages.
ELIOT What comes first? Can you see? Tell us. It is

5,800,000 rifles and carbines,
102,000 machine guns,
28,000 trench mortars,
53,000 field and heavy guns,
I cannot tell how many projectiles, mines and fuses,
13,000 aeroplanes,
24,000 aeroplane engines,
50,000 ammunition waggons,
now 55,000 army waggons,
11,000 field kitchens,
1,150 field bakeries.

What a time that took. Will it be he now? No,
Those are the golf club Captains, these the Scouts,
And now the *société gymnastique de Poissy*
And now come the Mayor and the Liverymen. Look
There he is now, look:
There is no interrogation in those eyes
Or in the hands, quiet over the horse's neck,
And the eyes watchful, waiting, perceiving, indifferent.
O hidden under the dove's wing, hidden in the turtle's
    breast,
Under the palmtree at noon, under the running water
At the still point of the turning world. O hidden.

Now they go up to the temple. Then the sacrifice.
Now come the virgins bearing urns, urns containing
Dust
Dust
Dust of dust, and now
Stone, bronze, stone, steel, stone, oakleaves, horses'
    heels

Over the paving.

That is all we could see. But how many eagles! and how
many trumpets!

(And Easter Day, we didn't get to the country,

So we took young Cyril to church. And they rang a
bell

And he said right out loud, *crumpets*.)

                    Don't throw away that sausage,

It'll come in handy. He's artful. Please, will you

Give us a light?

Light

Light

Et les soldats faisaient la haie? ILS LA FAISAIENT.

DIFFICULTIES OF A STATESMAN

Cry what shall I cry?

All flesh is grass: comprehending

The Companions of the Bath, the Knights of the British
Empire, the Cavaliers,

O Cavaliers! of the Legion of Honour,

The Order of the Black Eagle (1st and 2nd class),

And the Order of the Rising Sun.

Cry cry what shall I cry?

The first thing to do is to form the committees:

The consultative councils, the standing committees,
select committees and sub-committees.

One secretary will do for several committees.

What shall I cry?

Arthur Edward Cyril Parker is appointed telephone
operator

At a salary of one pound ten a week rising by annual
increments of five shillings

To two pounds ten a week; with a bonus of thirty
shillings at Christmas
And one week's leave a year.
A committee has been appointed to nominate a com-
mission of engineers
To consider the Water Supply.
A commission is appointed
For Public Works, primarily the question of rebuild-
ing the fortifications.
A commission is appointed
To confer with a Volscian commission
About perpetual peace: the fletchers and javelin-
makers and smiths
Have appointed a joint committee to protest against
the reduction of orders.
Meanwhile the guards shake dice on the marches
And the frogs (O Mantuan) croak in the marshes.
Fireflies flare against the faint sheet lightning,
What shall I cry?
Mother mother
Here is the row of family portraits, dingy busts, all
looking remarkably Roman,
Remarkably like each other, lit up successively by the
flare
Of a sweaty torchbearer, yawning.
O hidden under the   Hidden under the   Where the
dove's foot rested and locked for a moment,
A still moment, repose of noon, set under the upper
branches of noon's widest tree
Under the breast feather stirred by the small wind
after noon
There the cyclamen spreads its wings, there the
clematis droops over the lintel
O mother (not one of these busts all correctly inscribed)

I a tired head among these heads
Necks strong to bear them
Noses strong to break the wind
Mother
May we not be some time, almost now, together,
If the mactations, immolations, oblations, impetra-
      tions
Are now observed
May we not be
O hidden
Hidden in the stillness of noon, in the silent croaking
      night.
Come with the sweep of the little bat's wing, with the
      small flare of the firefly or lightning bug,
'Rising and falling, crowned with dust', the small
      creatures,
The small creatures chirp thinly through the dust, in
      the night.
O mother
What shall I cry?
We demand a committee, a representative committee,
      a committee of investigation
RESIGN   RESIGN   RESIGN

HAROLD MONRO

LIVING

Slow bleak awakening from the morning dream
Brings me in contact with the sudden day.
I am alive—this I.
I let my fingers move along my body.
Realisation warns them, and my nerves
Prepare their rapid messages and signals.
While Memory begins recording, coding,
Repeating; all the time Imagination
Mutters: You'll only die.

Here's a new day. O Pendulum move slowly!
My usual clothes are waiting on their peg.
I am alive—this I.
And in a moment Habit, like a crane,
Will bow its neck and dip its pulleyed cable,
Gathering me, my body, and our garment,
And swing me forth, oblivious of my question,
Into the daylight—why?

I think of all the others who awaken,
And wonder if they go to meet the morning
More valiantly than I;
Nor asking of this Day they will be living:
What have I done that I should be alive?
O, can I not forget that I am living?
How shall I reconcile the two conditions:
Living, and yet—to die?

Between the curtains the autumnal sunlight
With lean and yellow finger points me out;

The clock moans: Why? Why? Why?
But suddenly, as if without a reason,
Heart, Brain and Body, and Imagination
All gather in tumultuous joy together,
Running like children down the path of morning
To fields where they can play without a quarrel:
A country I'd forgotten, but remember,
And welcome with a cry.

HAROLD
MONRO

O cool glad pasture; living tree, tall corn,
Great cliff, or languid sloping sand, cold sea,
Waves; rivers curving: you, eternal flowers,
Give me content, while I can think of you:
Give me your living breath!
Back to your rampart, Death.

BITTER SANCTUARY

I

She lives in the porter's room; the plush is nicotined.
Clients have left their photos there to perish.
She watches through green shutters those who press
To reach unconsciousness.
She licks her varnished thin magenta lips,
She picks her foretooth with her finger nail,
She pokes her head out to greet new clients, or
To leave them (to what torture) waiting at the door.

II

Heat has locked the heavy earth,
Given strength to every sound.
He, where his life still holds him to the ground,
In anaesthesia, groaning for re-birth,

HAROLD Leans at the door.
MONRO From out the house there comes the dullest flutter;
       A lackey; and thin giggling from behind that shutter.

III

His lost eyes lean to find the number.
Follows his knuckled rap, and hesitating curse.
He cannot wake himself; he may not slumber;
While on the long white wall across the road
Drives the thin outline of a dwindling hearse.

IV

Now the door opens wide.

HE: 'Is there room inside?'
SHE: 'Are you past the bounds of pain?'
HE: 'May my body lie in vain
     Among the dreams I cannot keep!'
SHE: 'Let him drink the cup of sleep.'

V

Thin arms and ghostly hands; faint sky-blue eyes;
Long drooping lashes, lids like full-blown moons,
Clinging to any brink of floating skies:
What hope is there? What fear?—Unless to wake and
    see
Lingering flesh, or cold eternity.

O yet some face, half living, brings
Far gaze to him and croons—
SHE: 'You're white.   You are alone.
     Can you not approach my sphere?'
HE: 'I'm changing into stone.'
SHE: 'Would I were! Would *I* were!'
Then the white attendants fill the cup.

VI

In the morning through the world,
Watch the flunkeys bring the coffee;
Watch the shepherds on the downs,
Lords and ladies at their toilet,
Farmers, merchants, frothing towns.

But look how he, unfortunate, now fumbles
Through unknown chambers, and unheedful stumbles.
Can he evade the overshadowing night?
Are there not somewhere chinks of braided light?

VII

How do they leave who once are in those rooms?
Some may be found, they say, deeply asleep
In ruined tombs.
Some in white beds, with faces round them. Some
Wander the world, and never find a home.

ELM ANGEL

O, why?—
Only a dove can venture that reply.

Large lawns were laid as far as eye could reach;
Ocean lolled inward on a cool long beach;
A tall town motionless and breathless gleamed;
The dead half-listened and their mind half-dreamed;
Wrecks trembled deep in their perpetual tomb;
A quiet drooped upon the summer room.
Now a blue hooded honeysuckle lane,
A garden built of roses on the wane,
Sahara buried under naked sand,
A boy with large eyes from an eastern land,

HAROLD Muffled islands with hushed seas between
MONRO And one white temple glowing through the green;
Or, coming back, no place but only sound,
No elm that grew from any earthly ground,
But, heavenly throughout the atmosphere,
One ring dove cooing, crooning, cooing—Where?

CONRAD AIKEN

PRELUDE XIV

—You went to the verge, you say, and come back
    safely?
Some have not been so fortunate,—some have fallen.
Children go lightly there, from crag to crag,
And coign to coign,—where even the goat is wary,—
And make a sport of it. . . . They fling down pebbles,
Following, with eyes undizzied, the long curve,
The long slow outward curve, into the abyss,
As far as eye can follow; and they themselves
Turn back, unworried, to the here and now. . . .
But you have been there, too?—

                    —I saw at length
The space-defying pine, that on the last
Outjutting rock has cramped its powerful roots.
There stood I too: under that tree I stood:
My hand against its resinous bark: my face
Turned out and downward to the fourfold kingdom.
The wind roared from all quarters. The waterfall
Came down, it seemed, from Heaven. The mighty
    sound
Of pouring elements,—earth, air, and water,—
The cry of eagles, chatter of falling stones,—
These were the frightful language of that place.
I understood it ill, but understood.—

—You understood it? Tell me, then, its meaning.
It was an all, a nothing, or a something?
Chaos, or divine love, or emptiness?

CONRAD Water and earth and air and the sun's fire?
  AIKEN Or else, a question, simply?—

                              —Water and fire were there,
And air and earth; there too was emptiness;
All, and nothing, and something too, and love.
But these poor words, these squeaks of ours, in which
We strive to mimic, with strained throats and tongues,
The spawning and outrageous elements—
Alas, how paltry are they! For I saw—

—What did you see?

                    —I saw myself and God.
I saw the ruin in which godhead lives:
Shapeless and vast: the strewn wreck of the world:
Sadness unplumbed: misery without bound.
Wailing I heard, but also I heard joy.
Wreckage I saw, but also I saw flowers.
Hatred I saw, but also I saw love. . . .
And thus, I saw myself.

                    —And this alone?

—And this alone awaits you, when you dare
To that sheer verge where horror hangs, and tremble
Against the falling rock; and, looking down,
Search the dark kingdom. It is to self you come,—
And that is God. It is the seed of seeds:
Seed for disastrous and immortal worlds.

It is the answer that no question asked.

PRELUDE XXIX

CONRAD
AIKEN

What shall we do—what shall we think—what shall
    we say—?
Why, as the crocus does, on a March morning,
With just such shape and brightness; such fragility;
Such white and gold, and out of just such earth.
Or as the cloud does on the northeast wind—
Fluent and formless; or as the tree that withers.
What are we made of, strumpet, but of these?
Nothing. We are the sum of all these accidents—
Compounded all our days of idiot trifles,—
The this, the that, the other, and the next;
What x or y said, or old uncle thought;
Whether it rained or not, and at what hour;
Whether the pudding had two eggs or three,
And those we loved were ladies. . . . Were they
    ladies?
And did they read the proper books, and simper
With proper persons, at the proper teas?
O Christ and God and all deciduous things—
Let us void out this nonsense and be healed.

There is no doubt that we shall do, as always,
Just what the crocus does. There is no doubt
Your Helen of Troy is all that she has seen,—
All filth, all beauty, all honor and deceit.
The spider's web will hang in her bright mind,—
The dead fly die there doubly; and the rat
Find sewers to his liking. She will walk
In such a world as this alone could give—
This of the moment, this mad world of mirrors
And of corrosive memory. She will know
The lecheries of the cockroach and the worm,
The chemistry of the sunset, the foul seeds

CONRAD Laid by the intellect in the simple heart. . . .
AIKEN And knowing all these things, she will be she.

She will be also the sunrise on the grassblade—
But pay no heed to that. She will be also
The infinite tenderness of the voice of morning—
But pay no heed to that. She will be also
The grain of elmwood, and the ply of water,
Whirlings in sand and smoke, wind in the ferns,
The fixed bright eyes of dolls. . . . And this is all.

PRELUDE LVI

Rimbaud and Verlaine, precious pair of poets,
Genius in both (but what is genius?) playing
Chess on a marble table at an inn
With chestnut blossom falling in blond beer
And on their hair and between knight and bishop—
Sunlight squared between them on the chess-board
Cirrus in heaven, and a squeal of music
Blown from the leathern door of Ste. Sulpice—

Discussing, between moves, iamb and spondee
Anacoluthon and the open vowel
God the great peacock with his angel peacocks
And his dependent peacocks the bright stars:
Disputing too of fate as Plato loved it,
Or Sophocles, who hated and admired,
Or Socrates, who loved and was amused:

Verlaine puts down his pawn upon a leaf
And closes his long eyes, which are dishonest,
And says 'Rimbaud, there is one thing to do:
We must take rhetoric, and wring its neck! . . .'

Rimbaud considers gravely, moves his Queen;
And then removes himself to Timbuctoo.

CONRAD
AIKEN

And Verlaine dead,—with all his jades and mauves;
And Rimbaud dead in Marseilles with a vision,
His leg cut off, as once before his heart;
And all reported by a later lackey,
Whose virtue is his tardiness in time.

Let us describe the evening as it is:—
The stars disposed in heaven as they are:
Verlaine and Shakspere rotting, where they rot,
Rimbaud remembered, and too soon forgot;

Order in all things, logic in the dark;
Arrangement in the atom and the spark;
Time in the heart and sequence in the brain—

Such as destroyed Rimbaud and fooled Verlaine.
And let us then take godhead by the neck—

And strangle it, and with it, rhetoric.

EVENING

The light passes
from ridge to ridge,
from flower to flower—
the hypaticas, wide-spread
under the light
grow faint—
the petals reach inward,
the blue tips bend
toward the bluer heart
and the flowers are lost.

The cornel-buds are still white,
but shadows dart
from the cornel-roots—
black creeps from root to root
each leaf
cuts another leaf on the grass,
shadow seeks shadow,
then both leaf
and leaf-shadow are lost.

SEA ROSE

Rose, harsh rose,
marred and with stint of petals,
meagre flower, thin,
sparse of leaf,

more precious
than a wet rose
single on a stem—
you are caught in the drift.

Stunted, with small leaf,
you are flung on the sand,
you are lifted
in the crisp sand
that drives in the wind.

Can the spice-rose
drip such acrid fragrance
hardened in a leaf?

CHOROS FROM MORPHEUS

'Dream—dark-winged'

I

Give me your poppies,
poppies, one by one,
red poppies,
white ones,
red ones set by white;
I'm through with protestation;
my delight
knows nothing of the mind
or argument;
let me be done
with brain's intricacies;
your insight
has driven deeper
than the lordliest tome

H. D.

of Attic thought
or Cyrenian logic;
O strange, dark Morpheus,
covering me with wings,
you give the subtle fruit
Odysseus scorned
that left his townsmen fainting on the sands,
you bring the siren note,
the lotus-land;
O let me rest
at last,
at last,
at last;
your touch is sweeter
than the touch of Death;
O I am tired of measures
like deft oars;
the beat and ringing
of majestic song;
give me your poppies;
I would like along
hot rocks, listening;
still my ambition
that would rear and chafe
like chariot horses
waiting for the race;
let me forget
the spears of Marathon.

MARIANNE MOORE

THE STEEPLE-JACK

Dürer would have seen a reason for living
    in a town like this, with eight stranded whales
to look at; with the sweet sea air coming into your house
on a fine day, from water etched
    with waves as formal as the scales
on a fish.

One by one, in two's, in three's, the seagulls keep
    flying back and forth over the town clock,
or sailing around the lighthouse without moving the
        wings—
rising steadily with a slight
    quiver of the body—or flock
mewing where

a sea the purple of the peacock's neck is
    paled to greenish azure as Dürer changed
the pine green of the Tyrol to peacock blue and guinea
grey. You can see a twenty-five-
    pound lobster; and fishnets arranged
to dry. The

whirlwind fife-and-drum of the storm bends the salt
    marsh grass, disturbs stars in the sky and the
star on the steeple; it is a privilege to see so
much confusion. Disguised by what
    might seem austerity, the sea-
side flowers and

trees are favoured by the fog so that you have
    the tropics at first hand: the trumpet-vine,

fox-glove, giant snap-dragon, a salpiglossis that has
spots and stripes; morning-glories, gourds,
or moon-vines trained on fishing-twine
at the back

door. There are no banyans, frangipani, nor
    jack-fruit trees; nor an exotic serpent
life. Ring lizard and snake-skin for the foot, or
    crocodile;
but here they've cats, not cobras, to
    keep down the rats. The diffident
little newt

with white pin-dots on black horizontal spaced
    out bands lives here; yet there is nothing that
ambition can buy or take away. The college student
named Ambrose sits on the hill-side
    with his not-native books and hat
and sees boats

at sea progress white and rigid as if in
    a groove. Liking an elegance of which
the source is not bravado, he knows by heart the
    antique
sugar-bowl-shaped summer-house of
    interlacing slats, and the pitch
of the church

spire, not true, from which a man in scarlet lets
    down a rope as a spider spins a thread;
he might be part of a novel, but on the sidewalk a
sign says C. J. Poole, Steeple Jack,
    in black and white; and one in red
and white says

Danger. The church portico has four fluted
    columns, each a single piece of stone, made

modester by white-wash. This would be a fit haven for MARI-
ANNE
MOORE
waifs, children, animals, prisoners,
    and presidents who have repaid
sin-driven

senators by not thinking about them. There
    are a school-house, a post-office in a
store, fish-houses, hen-houses, a three-masted
        schooner on
the stocks. The hero, the student,
    the steeple-jack, each in his way,
is at home.

It could not be dangerous to be living
    in a town like this, of simple people,
who have a steeple-jack placing danger signs by the
        church
while he is gilding the solid-
    pointed star, which on a steeple
stands for hope.

BLACK EARTH

Openly, yes,
with the naturalness
    of the hippopotamus or the alligator
    when it climbs out on the bank to experience the

sun, I do these
things which I do, which please
    no one but myself. Now I breathe and now I am sub-
    merged; the blemishes stand up and shout when the
        object

MARI- in view was a
ANNE renaissance; shall I say
MOORE the contrary? The sediment of the river which
encrusts my joints, makes me very gray but I am
used

to it, it may
remain there; do away
with it and I am myself done away with, for the
patina of circumstance can but enrich what was

there to begin
with. This elephant-skin
which I inhabit, fibred over like the shell of
the cocoanut, this piece of black grass through
which no light

can filter—cut
into checkers by rut
upon rut of unpreventable experience—
it is a manual for the peanut-tongued and the

hairy-toed. Black
but beautiful, my back
is full of the history of power. Of power? What
is powerful and what is not? My soul shall never

be cut into
by a wooden spear; through-
out childhood to the present time, the unity of
life and death has been expressed by the
circumference

described by my
trunk; nevertheless I
perceive feats of strength to be inexplicable after
all; and I am on my guard; external poise, it

has its centre
well nurtured—we know
    where—in pride; but spiritual poise, it has its
        centre where?
    My ears are sensitized to more than the sound of

the wind. I see
and I hear, unlike the
    wandlike body of which one hears so much, which
        was made
    to see and not to see; to hear and not to hear;

that tree-trunk without
roots, accustomed to shout
    its own thoughts to itself like a shell, maintained
        intact
    by who knows what strange pressure of the atmo-
        sphere; that

spiritual
brother to the coral-
    plant, absorbed into which, the equable sapphire
        light
    becomes a nebulous green. The I of each is to

the I of each
a kind of fretful speech
    which sets a limit on itself; the elephant is
    black earth preceded by a tendril? Compared with
        those

phenomena
which vacillate like a
    translucence of the atmosphere, the elephant is
    that on which darts cannot strike decisively the first

MARI- time, a substance
ANNE needful as an instance
MOORE of the indestructibility of matter; it
has looked at the electricity and at the earth-

quake and is still
here; the name means thick. Will
depth be depth, thick skin be thick, to one who can
see no
beautiful element of unreason under it?

TO A STEAM ROLLER

The illustration
is nothing to you without the application.
You lack half wit. You crush all the particles down
into close conformity, and then walk back and
forth on them.

Sparkling chips of rock
are crushed down to the level of the parent block.
Were not 'impersonal judgment in aesthetic
matters, a metaphysical impossibility', you

might fairly achieve
it. As for butterflies, I can hardly conceive
of one's attending upon you, but to question
the congruence of the complement is vain, if it
exists.

TO A SNAIL

MARI-
ANNE
MOORE

If 'compression is the first grace of style',
you have it. Contractility is a virtue
as modesty is a virtue.
It is not the acquisition of any one thing
that is able to adorn,
or the incidental quality that occurs
as a concomitant of something well said,
that we value in style,
but the principle that is hid:
in the absence of feet, 'a method of conclusions';
'a knowledge of principles',
in the curious phenomenon of your occipital horn.

SILENCE

My father used to say,
'Superior people never make long visits,
have to be shown Longfellow's grave
or the glass flowers at Harvard.
Self-reliant like the cat—
that takes its prey to privacy,
the mouse's limp tail hanging like a shoelace from its
        mouth—
they sometimes enjoy solitude,
and can be robbed of speech
by speech which has delighted them.
The deepest feeling always shows itself in silence;
not in silence, but restraint'.
Nor was he insincere in saying, 'Make my house your
        inn'.
Inns are not residences.

TWO AT NORFOLK

Mow the grass in the cemetery, darkies,
Study the symbols and the requiescats,
But leave a bed beneath the myrtles.
This skeleton had a daughter and that, a son.

In his time, this one had little to speak of,
The softest word went gurrituck in his skull.
For him the moon was always in Scandinavia
And his daughter was a foreign thing.

And that one was never a man of heart.
The making of his son was one more duty.
When the music of the boy fell like a fountain,
He praised Johann Sebastian, as he should.

The dark shadows of the funereal magnolias
Are full of the songs of Jamanda and Carlotta;
The son and the daughter, who come to the darkness,
He for her burning breast and she for his arms.

And these two never meet in the air so full of summer
And touch each other, even touching closely,
Without an escape in the lapses of their kisses.
Make a bed and leave the iris in it.

TEA AT THE PALAZ OF HOON

WALLACE
STEVENS

Not less because in purple I descended
The western day through what you called
The loneliest air, not less was I myself.

What was the ointment sprinkled on my beard?
What were the hymns that buzzed beside my ears?
What was the sea whose tide swept through me there?

Out of my mind the golden ointment rained,
And my ears made the blowing hymns they heard.
I was myself the compass of that sea:

I was the world in which I walked, and what I saw
Or heard or felt came not but from myself;
And there I found myself more truly and more strange.

THE DEATH OF A SOLDIER

Life contracts and death is expected,
As in a season of autumn.
The soldier falls.

He does not become a three-days personage,
Imposing his separation,
Calling for pomp.

Death is absolute and without memorial,
As in a season of autumn,
When the wind stops,

When the wind stops and, over the heavens,
The clouds go, nevertheless,
In their direction.

WALLACE
STEVENS

THE EMPEROR OF ICE-CREAM

Call the roller of big cigars,
The muscular one, and bid him whip
In kitchen cups concupiscent curds.
Let the wenches dawdle in such dress
As they are used to wear, and let the boys
Bring flowers in last month's newspapers.
Let be be finale of seem.
The only emperor is the emperor of ice-cream.

Take from the dresser of deal,
Lacking the three glass knobs, that sheet
On which she embroidered fantails once
And spread it so as to cover her face.
If her horny feet protrude, they come
To show how cold she is, and dumb.
Let the lamp affix its beam.
The only emperor is the emperor of ice-cream.

VACHEL LINDSAY

GENERAL WILLIAM BOOTH ENTERS INTO HEAVEN

Booth led boldly with his big bass drum.
(Are you washed in the blood of the Lamb?)
The Saints smiled gravely and they said: 'He's come.'
(Are you washed in the blood of the Lamb?)
Walking lepers following, rank on rank,
Lurching bravos from the ditches dank,
Drabs from the alleyways and drug fiends pale—
Minds still passion-ridden, soul-powers frail:
Vermin-eaten saints with moldy breath,
Unwashed legions with the ways of Death—
(Are you washed in the blood of the Lamb?)

Every slum had sent its half-a-score
The round world over. (Booth had groaned for more.)
Every banner that the wide world flies
Bloomed with glory and transcendent dyes.
Big-voiced lasses made their banjos bang,
Tranced, fanatical they shrieked and sang:
'Are you washed in the blood of the Lamb?'
Hallelujah! It was queer to see
Bull-necked convicts with that land make free.
Loons with trumpets blowed a blare, blare, blare
On, on upward thro' the golden air!
(Are you washed in the blood of the Lamb?)

Booth died blind and still by faith he trod,
Eyes still dazzled by the ways of God.
Booth led boldly, and he looked the chief

Eagle countenance in sharp relief,
Beard a-flying, air of high command
Unabated in that holy land.

Jesus came from out the court-house door,
Stretched his hands above the passing poor.
Booth saw not, but led his queer ones there
Round and round the mighty court-house square.
Then, in an instant all that blear review
Marched on spotless, clad in raiment new.
The lame were straightened, withered limbs uncurled
And blind eyes opened on a new, sweet world.

Drabs and vixens in a flash made whole!
Gone was the weasel-head, the snout, the jowl!
Sages and sibyls now, and athletes clean,
Rulers of empires, and of forests green!
The hosts were sandalled, and their wings were fire!
(Are you washed in the blood of the Lamb?)
But their noise played havoc with the angel-choir.
(Are you washed in the blood of the Lamb?)

Oh, shout Salvation! It was good to see
Kings and Princes by the Lamb set free.
The banjos rattled and the tambourines
Jing-jing-jingled in the hands of Queens.

And when Booth halted by the curb for prayer
He saw his Master thro' the flag-filled air.
Christ came gently with a robe and crown
For Booth the soldier, while the throng knelt down.
He saw King Jesus. They were face to face,
And he knelt a-weeping in that holy place.
Are you washed in the blood of the Lamb?

D. H. LAWRENCE

END OF ANOTHER HOME HOLIDAY

When shall I see the half-moon sink again
Behind the black sycamore at the end of the garden?
When will the scent of the dim white phlox
Creep up the wall to me, and in at my open window?

Why is it, the long, slow stroke of the midnight bell
    (Will it never finish the twelve?)
Falls again and again on my heart with a heavy
    reproach?

The moon-mist is over the village, out of the mist
    speaks the bell,
And all the little roofs of the village bow low, pitiful,
    beseeching, resigned.
—Speak, you my home! What is it I don't do well?

Ah home, suddenly I love you
As I hear the sharp clean trot of a pony down the road,
Succeeding sharp little sounds dropping into silence
Clear upon the long-drawn hoarseness of a train across
    the valley.

\   .   .   .   .

The light has gone out, from under my mother's door.
      That she should love me so!—
      She, so lonely, greying now!
      And I leaving her,
      Bent on my pursuits!

      Love is the great Asker.
      The sun and the rain do not ask the secret

Of the time when the grain struggles down
    in the dark.
The moon walks her lonely way without
    anguish,
Because no-one grieves over her departure.

Forever, ever by my shoulder pitiful love will linger,
Crouching as little houses crouch under the mist when
    I turn.
Forever, out of the mist, the church lifts up a reproach-
    ful finger,
Pointing my eyes in wretched defiance where love
    hides her face to mourn.

    Oh! but the rain creeps down to wet the grain
    That struggles alone in the dark,
    And asking nothing, patiently steals back again!
    The moon sets forth o' nights
    To walk the lonely, dusky heights
    Serenely, with steps unswerving;
    Pursued by no sigh of bereavement,
    No tears of love unnerving
    Her constant tread:
    While ever at my side,
    Frail and sad, with grey, bowed head,
    The beggar-woman, the yearning-eyed
    Inexorable love goes lagging.

The wild young heifer, glancing distraught,
With a strange new knocking of life at her side
    Runs seeking a loneliness.
The little grain draws down the earth, to hide.
Nay, even the slumberous egg, as it labours under
    the shell

Patiently to divide and self-divide,
Asks to be hidden, and wishes nothing to tell.

But when I draw the scanty cloak of silence over my
eyes
Piteous love comes peering under the hood;
Touches the clasp with trembling fingers, and tries
To put her ear to the painful sob of my blood;
While her tears soak through to my breast,
Where they burn and cauterise.

.   .   .   .

The moon lies back and reddens.
In the valley a corncrake calls
Monotonously,
With a plaintive, unalterable voice, that
deadens
My confident activity;
With a hoarse, insistent request that falls
Unweariedly, unweariedly,
Asking something more of me,
Yet more of me.

SONG OF A MAN WHO HAS COME
THROUGH

Not I, not I, but the wind that blows through me!
A fine wind is blowing the new direction of Time.
If only I let it bear me, carry me, if only it carry me!
If only I am sensitive, subtle, oh, delicate, a winged
gift!
If only, most lovely of all, I yield myself and am
borrowed

153

By the fine, fine wind that takes its course through the
chaos of the world
Like a fine, an exquisite chisel, a wedge-blade
inserted;
If only I am keen and hard like the sheer tip of a wedge
Driven by invisible blows,
The rock will split, we shall come at the wonder, we
shall find the Hesperides.

Oh, for the wonder that bubbles into my soul,
I would be a good fountain, a good well-head,
Would blur no whisper, spoil no expression.

What is the knocking?
What is the knocking at the door in the night?
It is somebody wants to do us harm.

No, no, it is the three strange angels.
Admit them, admit them.

SNAKE

A snake came to my water-trough
On a hot, hot day, and I in pyjamas for the heat,
To drink there.

In the deep, strange-scented shade of the great dark
carob-tree
I came down the steps with my pitcher
And must wait, must stand and wait, for there he was
at the trough before me.

He reached down from a fissure in the earth-wall in the
gloom
And trailed his yellow-brown slackness soft-bellied
down, over the edge of the stone trough

And rested his throat upon the stone bottom,
And where the water had dripped from the tap, in a
    small clearness,
He sipped with his straight mouth,
Softly drank through his straight gums, into his slack
    long body,
Silently.

Someone was before me at my water-trough,
And I, like a second comer, waiting.

He lifted his head from his drinking, as cattle do,
And looked at me vaguely, as drinking cattle do,
And flickered his two-forked tongue from his lips, and
    mused a moment,
And stooped and drank a little more,
Being earth-brown, earth-golden from the burning
    bowels of the earth
On the day of Sicilian July, with Etna smoking.

The voice of my education said to me
He must be killed,
For in Sicily the black, black snakes are innocent, the
    gold are venomous.

And voices in me said, If you were a man
You would take a stick and break him now, and finish
    him off.

But must I confess how I liked him,
How glad I was he had come like a guest in quiet, to
    drink at my water-trough
And depart peaceful, pacified, and thankless,
Into the burning bowels of this earth?

Was it cowardice, that I dared not kill him?
Was it perversity, that I longed to talk to him?

155

D. H. Was it humility, to feel so honoured?
LAW- I felt so honoured.
RENCE And yet those voices:
If you were not afraid, you would kill him!

And truly I was afraid, I was most afraid,
But even so, honoured still more
That he should seek my hospitality
From out the dark door of the secret earth.

He drank enough
And lifted his head, dreamily, as one who has drunken,
And flickered his tongue like a forked night on the air, so
    black,
Seeming to lick his lips,
And looked around like a god, unseeing, into the air,
And slowly turned his head,
And slowly, very slowly, as if thrice adream,
Proceeded to draw his slow length curving round
And climb again the broken bank of my wall-face.

And as he put his head into that dreadful hole,
And as he slowly drew up, snake-easing his shoulders,
    and entered farther,
A sort of horror, a sort of protest against his with-
    drawing into that horrid black hole,
Deliberately going into the blackness, and slowly
    drawing himself after,
Overcame me now his back was turned.

I looked round, I put down my pitcher,
I picked up a clumsy log
And threw it at the water-trough with a clatter.

I think it did not hit him,
But suddenly that part of him that was left behind
    convulsed in undignified haste,

Writhed like lightning, and was gone
Into the black hole, the earth-lipped fissure in the
    wall-front,
At which, in the intense still noon, I stared with
    fascination.

And immediately I regretted it.
I thought how paltry, how vulgar, what a mean act!
I despised myself and the voices of my accursed human
    education.

And I thought of the albatross,
And I wished he would come back, my snake.

For he seemed to me again like a king,
Like a king in exile, uncrowned in the underworld,
Now due to be crowned again.

And so, I missed my chance with one of the lords
Of life.
And I have something to expiate;
A pettiness.

                                        Taormina

BAVARIAN GENTIANS

Not every man has gentians in his house
in Soft September, at slow, Sad Michaelmas.

Bavarian gentians, big and dark, only dark
darkening the day-time torch-like with the smoking
    blueness of Pluto's gloom,
ribbed and torch-like, with their blaze of darkness
    spread blue
down flattening into points, flattened under the sweep
    of white day

torch-flower of the blue-smoking darkness, Pluto's
dark-blue daze,
black lamps from the halls of Dio, burning dark blue,
giving off darkness, blue darkness, as Demeter's pale
lamps give off light,
lead me then, lead me the way.

Reach me a gentian, give me a torch
let me guide myself with the blue, forked torch of this
flower
down the darker and darker stairs, where blue is
darkened on blueness.
even where Persephone goes, just now, from the
frosted September
to the sightless realm where darkness is awake upon the
dark
and Persephone herself is but a voice
or a darkness invisible enfolded in the deeper dark
of the arms Plutonic, and pierced with the passion of
dense gloom,
among the splendour of torches of darkness, shedding
darkness on the lost bride and her groom.

ISAAC ROSENBERG

RETURNING, WE HEAR THE LARKS

Sombre the night is:
And, though we have our lives, we know
What sinister threat lurks there.

Dragging these anguished limbs, we only know
This poison-blasted track opens on our camp—
On a little safe sleep.

But hark! Joy—joy—strange joy.
Lo! Heights of night ringing with unseen larks:
Music showering on our upturned listening faces.

Death could drop from the dark
As easily as song—
But song only dropped,
Like a blind man's dreams on the sand
By dangerous tides;
Like a girl's dark hair, for she dreams no ruin lies there,
Or her kisses where a serpent hides.

THE BURNING OF THE TEMPLE

Fierce wrath of Solomon,
Where sleepest thou? O see,
The fabric which thou won
Earth and ocean to give thee—
O look at the red skies.

159

Or hath the sun plunged down?
What is this molten gold—
These thundering fires blown
Through heaven, where the smoke rolled?
Again the great king dies.

His dreams go out in smoke.
His days he let not pass
And sculptured here are broke,
Are charred as the burnt grass,
Gone as his mouth's last sighs.

DEAD MAN'S DUMP

The plunging limbers over the shattered track
Racketed with their rusty freight,
Stuck out like many crowns of thorns,
And the rusty stakes like sceptres old
To stay the flood of brutish men
Upon our brothers dear.

The wheels lurched over sprawled dead
But pained them not, though their bones crunched;
Their shut mouths made no moan.
They lie there huddled, friend and foeman,
Man born of man, and born of woman;
And shells go crying over them
From night till night and now.

Earth has waited for them,
All the time of their growth
Fretting for their decay:
Now she has them at last!
In the strength of their strength
Suspended—stopped and held.

What fierce imaginings their dark souls lit?
Earth! Have they gone into you?
Somewhere they must have gone,
And flung on your hard back
Is their souls' sack,
Emptied of God-ancestralled essences.
Who hurled them out? Who hurled?

None saw their spirits' shadow shake the grass,
Or stood aside for the half used life to pass
Out of those doomed nostrils and the doomed mouth,
When the swift iron burning bee
Drained the wild honey of their youth.

What of us who, flung on the shrieking pyre,
Walk, our usual thoughts untouched,
Our lucky limbs as on ichor fed,
Immortal seeming ever?
Perhaps when the flames beat loud on us,
A fear may choke in our veins
And the startled blood may stop.

The air is loud with death,
The dark air spurts with fire,
The explosions ceaseless are.
Timelessly now, some minutes past,
These dead strode time with vigorous life,
Till the shrapnel called 'An end!'
But not to all. In bleeding pangs
Some borne on stretchers dreamed of home,
Dear things, war-blotted from their hearts.

A man's brains splattered on
A stretcher-bearer's face;
His shook shoulders slipped their load,
But when they bent to look again

The drowning soul was sunk too deep
For human tenderness.

They left this dead with the older dead,
Stretched at the cross roads.

Burnt black by strange decay
Their sinister faces lie,
The lid over each eye;
The grass and coloured clay
More motion have than they,
Joined to the great sunk silences.

Here is one not long dead.
His dark hearing caught our far wheels,
And the choked soul stretched weak hands
To reach the living word the far wheels said;
The blood-dazed intelligence beating for light,
Crying through the suspense of the far torturing
        wheels
Swift for the end to break
Or the wheels to break,
Cried as the tide of the world broke over his sight,
'Will they come? Will they ever come?'
Even as the mixed hoofs of the mules,
The quivering-bellied mules,
And the rushing wheels all mixed
With his tortured upturned sight.

So we crashed round the bend,
We heard his weak scream,
We heard his very last sound,
And our wheels grazed his dead face.

BREAK OF DAY IN THE TRENCHES

ISAAC
ROSEN-
BERG

The darkness crumbles away—
It is the same old druid Time as ever.
Only a live thing leaps my hand—
A queer sardonic rat—
As I pull the parapet's poppy
To stick behind my ear.
Droll rat, they would shoot you if they knew
Your cosmopolitan sympathies
(And God knows what antipathies).
Now you have touched this English hand
You will do the same to a German—
Soon, no doubt, if it be your pleasure
To cross the sleeping green between.
It seems you inwardly grin as you pass
Strong eyes, fine limbs, haughty athletes
Less chanced than you for life,
Bonds to the whims of murder,
Sprawled in the bowels of the earth,
The torn fields of France.
What do you see in our eyes
At the shrieking iron and flame
Hurled through still heavens?
What quaver—what heart aghast?
Poppies whose roots are in man's veins
Drop, and are ever dropping;
But mine in my ear is safe,
Just a little white with the dust.

From MOSES: A PLAY

The Young Hebrew speaks:

Yesterday as I lay nigh dead with toil
Underneath the hurtling crane oiled with our blood,
Thinking to end all and let the crane crush me,
He came by and bore me into the shade:
O, what a furnace roaring in his blood
Thawed my congealed sinews and tingled my own
Raging through me like a strong cordial.
He spoke! Since yesterday
Am I not larger grown?
I've seen men hugely shapen in soul,
Of such unhuman shaggy male turbulence
They tower in foam miles from our neck-strained
        sight,
And to their shop only heroes come;
But all were cripples to this speed
Constrained to the stables of flesh.
I say there is a famine in ripe harvest
When hungry giants come as guests:
Come knead the hills and ocean into food,
There is none for him.
The streaming vigours of his blood erupting
From his halt tongue are like an anger thrust
Out of a madman's piteous craving for
A monstrous balked perfection.

WILFRED OWEN

FROM MY DIARY, JULY 1914

Leaves
    Murmuring by myriads in the shimmering trees.
Lives
    Wakening with wonder in the Pyrenees.
Birds
    Cheerily chirping in the early day.
Bards
    Singing of summer scything thro' the hay.
Bees
    Shaking the heavy dews from bloom and frond.
Boys
    Bursting the surface of the ebony pond.
Flashes
    Of swimmers carving thro' the sparkling cold.
Fleshes
    Gleaming with wetness to the morning gold.
A mead
    Bordered about with warbling water brooks.
A maid
    Laughing the love-laugh with me; proud of looks.
The heat
    Throbbing between the upland and the peak.
Her heart
    Quivering with passion to my pressed cheek.
Braiding
    Of floating flames across the mountain brow.
Brooding
    Of stillness; and a sighing of the bough.

Of leaflets in the gloom; soft petal-showers;

Expanding with the starr'd nocturnal flowers.

EXPOSURE

Our brains ache, in the merciless iced east winds that
knive us . . .
Wearied we keep awake because the night is silent . . .
Low, drooping flares confuse our memory of the
salient . . .
Worried by silence, sentries whisper, curious,
nervous,
But nothing happens.

Watching, we hear the mad gusts tugging on the wire,
Like twitching agonies of men among its brambles.
Northward, incessantly, the flickering gunnery
rumbles,
Far off, like a dull rumour of some other war.
What are we doing here?

The poignant misery of dawn begins to grow . . .
We only know war lasts, rain soaks, and clouds sag
stormy.
Dawn massing in the east her melancholy army
Attacks once more in ranks on shivering ranks of gray,
But nothing happens.

Sudden successive flights of bullets streak the silence.
Less deadly than the air that shudders black with snow,
With sidelong flowing flakes that flock, pause, and
renew,

166

We watch them wandering up and down the wind's
    nonchalance,
        But nothing happens.

WILFRED
OWEN

Pale flakes with fingering stealth come feeling for our
    faces—
We cringe in holes, back on forgotten dreams, and
    stare, snow-dazed,
Deep into grassier ditches. So we drowse, sun-dozed,
Littered with blossoms trickling where the blackbird
    fusses.
        Is it that we are dying?

Slowly our ghosts drag home: glimpsing the sunk fires,
    glozed
With crusted dark-red jewels; crickets jingle there;
For hours the innocent mice rejoice: the house is
    theirs;
Shutters and doors, all closed: on us the doors are
    closed,—
        We turn back to our dying.

Since we believe not otherwise can kind fires burn;
Nor ever suns smile true on child, or field, or fruit.
For God's invincible spring our love is made afraid;
Therefore, not loath, we lie out here; therefore were
    born,
        For love of God seems dying.

To-night, His frost will fasten on this mud and us,
Shrivelling many hands, puckering foreheads crisp.
The burying-party, picks and shovels in their shaking
    grasp,
Pause over half-known faces. All their eyes are ice,
        But nothing happens.

Red lips are not so red
  As the stained stones kissed by the English dead.
Kindness of wooed and wooer
Seems shame to their love pure.
O Love, your eyes lose lure
  When I behold eyes blinded in my stead!

Your slender attitude
  Trembles not exquisite like limbs knife-skewed,
Rolling and rolling there
Where God seems not to care;
Till the fierce Love they bear
  Cramps them in death's extreme decrepitude.

Your voice sings not so soft,—
  Though even as wind murmuring through raftered
    loft,—
Your dear voice is not dear,
Gentle, and evening clear,
As theirs whom none now hear,
  Now earth has stopped their piteous mouths that
    coughed.

Heart, you were never hot,
  Nor large, nor full like hearts made great with shot;
And though your hand be pale,
Paler are all which trail
Your cross through flame and hail:
  Weep, you may weep, for you may touch them not.

MENTAL CASES

WILFRED
OWEN

Who are these? Why sit they here in twilight?
Wherefore rock they, purgatorial shadows,
Drooping tongues from jaws that slob their relish,
Baring teeth that leer like skulls' teeth wicked?
Stroke on stroke of pain,—but what slow panic,
Gouged these chasms round their fretted sockets?
Ever from their hair and through their hands' palms
Misery swelters. Surely we have perished
Sleeping, and walk hell; but who these hellish?

—These are men whose minds the Dead have ravished.
Memory fingers in their hair of murders,
Multitudinous murders they once witnessed.
Wading sloughs of flesh these helpless wander,
Treading blood from lungs that had loved laughter.
Always they must see these things and hear them,
Batter of guns and shatter of flying muscles,
Carnage incomparable, and human squander,
Rucked too thick for these men's extrication.

Therefore still their eyeballs shrink tormented
Back into their brains, because on their sense
Sunlight seems a blood-smear; night comes blood-
        black;
Dawn breaks open like a wound that bleeds afresh
—Thus their heads wear this hilarious, hideous,
Awful falseness of set-smiling corpses.
—Thus their hands are plucking at each other;
Picking at the rope-knouts of their scourging;
Snatching after us who smote them, brother,
Pawing us who dealt them war and madness.

FUTILITY

Move him in the sun—
Gently its touch awoke him once,
At home, whispering of fields unsown.
Always it woke him, even in France,
Until this morning and this snow.
If anything might rouse him now
The kind old sun will know.

Think how it wakes the seeds,—
Woke, once, the clays of a cold star.
Are limbs, so dear-achieved, are sides,
Full-nerved—still warm—too hard to stir?
Was it for this the clay grew tall?
—O what made fatuous sunbeams toil
To break earth's sleep at all?

ANTHEM FOR DOOMED YOUTH

What passing-bells for these who die as cattle?
    Only the monstrous anger of the guns.
    Only the stuttering rifles' rapid rattle
Can patter out their hasty orisons.
No mockeries for them from prayers or bells,
    Nor any voice of mourning save the choirs,—
The shrill, demented choirs of wailing shells;
    And bugles calling for them from sad shires.

What candles may be held to speed them all?
    Not in the hands of boys, but in their eyes
Shall shine the holy glimmers of good-byes.
    The pallor of girls' brows shall be their pall;
Their flowers the tenderness of silent minds,
And each slow dusk a drawing-down of blinds.

STRANGE MEETING

WILFRED
OWEN

It seemed that out of battle I escaped
Down some profound dull tunnel, long since scooped
Through granites which titanic wars had groined.
Yet also there encumbered sleepers groaned,
Too fast in thought or death to be bestirred.
Then, as I probed them, one sprang up, and stared
With piteous recognition in fixed eyes,
Lifting distressful hands as if to bless.
And by his smile, I knew that sullen hall,
By his dead smile I knew we stood in Hell.
With a thousand pains that vision's face was grained;
Yet no blood reached there from the upper ground,
And no guns thumped, or down the flues made moan.
'Strange friend', I said, 'here is no cause to mourn.'
'None', said the other, 'save the undone years,
The hopelessness. Whatever hope is yours,
Was my life also; I went hunting wild
After the wildest beauty in the world,
Which lies not calm in eyes, or braided hair,
But mocks the steady running of the hour,
And if it grieves, grieves richlier than here.
For by my glee might many men have laughed,
And of my weeping something had been left,
Which must die now. I mean the truth untold,
The pity of war, the pity war distilled.
Now men will go content with what we spoiled.
Or, discontent, boil bloody, and be spilled.
They will be swift with swiftness of the tigress,
None will break ranks, though nations trek from
         progress.
Courage was mine, and I had mystery,
Wisdom was mine, and I had mastery;

WILFRED
OWEN To miss the march of this retreating world
Into vain citadels that are not walled.
>   Then, when much blood had clogged their chariot-
>   wheels
>   I would go up and wash them from sweet wells,
>   Even with truths that lie too deep for taint.
>   I would have poured my spirit without stint
>   But not through wounds; not on the cess of war.
>   Foreheads of men have bled where no wounds were.
>   I am the enemy you killed, my friend.
>   I knew you in this dark; for so you frowned
>   Yesterday through me as you jabbed and killed.
>   I parried; but my hands were loath and cold.
>   Let us sleep now. . . .'

HERBERT READ

MY COMPANY

Foule! Ton âme entière est debout
dans mon corps.

I

You became
In many acts and quiet observances
A body and a soul, entire.

I cannot tell
What time your life became mine:
Perhaps when one summer night
We halted on the roadside
In the starlight only,
And you sang your sad home-songs,
Dirges which I standing outside you
Coldly condemned.

Perhaps, one night, descending cold
When rum was mighty acceptable,
And my doling gave birth to sensual gratitude.

And then our fights: we've fought together
Compact, unanimous;
And I have felt the pride of leadership.

In many acts and quiet observances
You absorbed me:
Until one day I stood eminent
And saw you gathered round me,
Uplooking,

And about you a radiance that seemed to beat
With variant glow and to give
Grace to our unity.

But, God! I know that I'll stand
Someday in the loneliest wilderness,
Someday my heart will cry
For the soul that has been, but that now
Is scattered with the winds,
Deceased and devoid.

I know that I'll wander with a cry:
'O beautiful men, O men I loved,
O whither are you gone, my company?'

2

My men go wearily
With their monstrous burdens.

They bear wooden planks
And iron sheeting
Through the area of death.

When a flare curves through the sky
They rest immobile.

Then on again,
Sweating and blaspheming—
'Oh, bloody Christ!'

My men, my modern Christs,
Your bloody agony confronts the world.

3

A man of mine
          lies on the wire.
It is death to fetch his soulless corpse.

A man of mine
     lies on the wire;
And he will rot
And first his lips
The worms will eat.

It is not thus I would have him kissed,
But with the warm passionate lips
Of his comrade here.

4

I can assume
A giant attitude and godlike mood,
And then detachedly regard
All riots, conflicts and collisions.

The men I've lived with
Lurch suddenly into a far perspective;
They distantly gather like a dark cloud of birds.
In the autumn sky.

Urged by some unanimous
Volition or fate,
Clouds clash in opposition;
The sky quivers, the dead descend;
Earth yawns.

They are all of one species.

From my giant attitude,
In godlike mood,
I laugh till space is filled
With hellish merriment.

Then again I assume
My human docility,
Bow my head
And share their doom.

CRANACH

But once upon a time
the oakleaves and the wild boars
Antonio Antonio
the old wound is bleeding.

We are in Silvertown
we have come here with a modest ambition
to know a little bit about the river
eating cheese and pickled onions on a terrace by the
Thames.

Sweet Thames! the ferry glides across your bosom
like Leda's swan.
The factories ah slender graces
sly naked damsels nodding their downy plumes.

THE FALCON AND THE DOVE

I

This high-caught hooded Reason broods upon my
wrist,
Fettered by a so tenuous leash of steel.
We are bound for the myrtle marshes, many leagues
away,
And have a fair expectation of quarry.

Over the laggard dove, inclining to green boscage
Hovers this intentional doom—till the unsullied sky
    receives
A precipitation of shed feathers
And the swifter fall of wounded wings.

3

Will the plain aye echo with that loud *hullallo!*
Or retain an impress of our passage?
We have caught Beauty in a wild foray
And now the falcon is hooded and comforted away.

A NORTHERN LEGION

Bugle calls coiling through the rocky valley
have found echoes in the eagles' cries:
an outrage is done on anguished men
now men die and death is no deedful glory.

Eleven days this legion forced the ruined fields, the
burnt homesteads and empty garths, the broken arches
of bridges: desolation moving like a shadow before
    them, a
rain of ashes. Endless their anxiety

marching into a northern darkness: approaching
a narrow defile, the waters falling fearfully
the clotting menace of shadows and all the multiple
instruments of death in ambush against them.

The last of the vanguard sounds his doleful note.
The legion now is lost. None will follow.

TIME REGAINED

The limbs remember blood and fire:
a hurt that's done may in the mind
sink and lose identity;

for the mind has reasons of its own
for covering with an eyeless mask
marks of mortality. ·

The limbs remember fire and joy
and flesh to flesh is benison
of entity;

but the mind has reasons of its own
for circumventing life and love's
sodality.

THE SEVEN SLEEPERS

The seven sleepers ere they left
the light and colour of the earth
the seven sleepers they did cry
(banishing their final fears):

'Beauty will not ever fade.
To our cavern we retire
doomed to sleep ten thousand years.
Roll the rock across the gap

Then forget us; we are quiet:
stiff and cold our bodies lie;
Earth itself shall stir ere we
visit Earth's mortality.

Beauty when we wake will be
a solitude on land and sea.'

THE ANALYSIS OF LOVE

HERBERT
READ

Else a great Prince in prison lies.

JOHN DONNE

I

I would have my own vision
    The world's vision:
The beauty settled in my mind
    A lamp in a busy street.

Yet these activities are too intimate,
    Made for a solitary sense:
However builded the emotion,
    The imagination's mute.

Could voice join mind's eye and scream
    Its vision out
Then the world would halt its toil,
    Passionless, time unreal.

2

Night palliates
    The ragged ridge of things;
The stars, however minute, are intense
    And pierce beyond the reckoning brain.

The stars and the dark palliation
    Are not indwelling
When driven lust has dark dominion
    In the mind's eclipse.

Yet sleep is relentless, extinguishing all
    Under its cone of annihilation;
And in the fresh and cool morning
    The lusting man is lost.

179

And lust is a finite thing,
    Deftly to be sized by the passionless mind.
Lust gone, other elements exist
    Wrought in the body's being.

The measuring mind can appraise
    An earthen grace;
The idiot's chatter
    Analyses into experience.

But your appeal is imperceptible
    As ultimate atoms
And the fast matrix
    Of all within the human universe.

4

There are moments when I see your mind
    Lapsed in your sex;
When one particular deployment
    Is the reflex of incomplete attainment.

These moments vanish
    Like lamps at daybreak:
The wide and even light
    Is kind and real.

And then you are universal;
    I too: our minds,
Not cramped by figured thought
    Unite in the impersonal beauty we possess.

5

Since you are finite you will never find
    The hidden source of the mind's emotion;

It is a pool, secret in dusk and dawn,
    Deep in the chartless forest life has grown.

Since you are blind you do not see
    The thirsting beasts peer from gnarled roots,
And creep to the brink, at noon,
    To lap with rough tongues, rippling the burnished
        serenity.

—This mind which is collected
    From many tricklings, of dew and rain,
Of which you are the chief
    And freshest in its depths.

6

You will not drive me to the anguish of love
    By any torture of this faith,
Converting to the corrupted semblance of despair
    The still evidence of my look;

But by the triumph of those traits—
    Their multiplication to excess—
Which mark the frailties germinant
    In a mind emotion-bound.

Not that I fear your capture
    In human littlenesses;
These are drops we can absorb
    In the fount and flow of a passionless mood.

7

The teased fibrils of reason
    Weave vainly to dam
Some bank against the giant flood
    Of this emotion.

Waves' and winds' erosion
Crumbles granitic cliffs,
Æonly obliterating
   The earth's known visage.

The multiple striving of the human race
   Wins slowly mind's conquest
Of brutal foes; or is the supreme foe
   This hope, deluding?

8

When you have totalled this life
   And got the vision complete:
When you have seen a central horror
   Blacking out the sun's gift—

Take me: englobe my soul
   And spin it on an axis;
Set about me ringed planets
   And diverse atmospheres.

And in that world
   Lacking the imperfections of this,
Live boldly, plant sapling trees,
   Expecting a burden of fruit.

9

You will say that I am in the scheme of things,
   A unit in the crumbling earth;
Trees are barren:
   Chance I'm a barren tree.

Link me with circumstances if you must,
   But live to triumph all the same:
We'll be insensate when the whirl
   Of circumstance is past.

You'll not avoid the avalanche;
　　But parasitic on my soul
You run, beat, rebound and throb
　　In world descent.

10

Nature has perpetual tears
　　In drooping boughs,
And everywhere inanimate death
　　Is immemorial.

But I have naught that will express
　　The grief I feel
When men and moods combine to show
　　The end of this—

This mental ecstasy all spent
　　In disuniting death;
And the years that spread
　　Oblivion on our zest.

BEATA L'ALMA

Beata l'alma, ove non corre tempo.
MICHELANGELO

I

Time ends when vision sees its lapse in
　　　liberty. The seven
sleepers quit their den and wild
　　　　lament-
tions fill our voiceless bodies. Echoes only are.

183

You will never understand the mind's
           misanthropy, nor see
     that all is foul and fit to
           screech in.
It is an eye's anarchy: men are ghoulish stumps

     and the air a river of opaque
           filth. God! I cannot see
     to design these stark reaches, these
           bulging
contours pressed against me in the maddening dark.

     A blindman's buff and no distilling
           of song for the woeful
     scenes of agony. Never
           will rest
the mind an instant in its birdlike flutterings.

     Could I impress my voice on the plas-
           tic darkness, or lift an
     inviolate lanthorn from
           a ship
in the storm I might have ease. But why? No fellows

     would answer my hullallo, and my
           lanthorn would lurch on the
     mast till it dipped under the
           wet waves
and the hissing darkness healed the wide wound of
     light.

     A cynic race—to bleak ecstasies
           we are driven by our
     sombre destiny. Men's shouts
           are not
glad enough to echo in our groined hearts. We know

184

war and its dead, and famine's bleached bones;
      black rot overreaching
the silent pressure of life
         in fronds
of green ferns and in the fragile shell of white flesh.

HERBERT
READ

2

New children must be born of gods in
      a deathless land, where the
uneroded rocks bound clear
         from cool
glassy tarns, and no flaw is in mind or flesh.

Sense and image they must refashion—
      they will not recreate
love: love ends in hate; they will
         not use
words: words lie. The structure of events alone is

comprehensible and to single
      perceptions communic-
 ation is not essential.
         Art ends;
the individual world alone is valid

and that gives ease. The water is still;
      the rocks are hard and veined,
metalliferous, yielding
         an ore
of high worth. In the sky the unsullied sun lake.

JOHN CROWE RANSOM

VISION BY SWEETWATER

Go and ask Robin to bring the girls over
To Sweetwater, said my Aunt; and that was why
It was like a dream of ladies sweeping by
The willows, clouds, deep meadowgrass, and the
    river.

Robin's sisters and my Aunt's lily daughter
Laughed and talked, and tinkled light as wrens
If there were a little colony all hens
To go walking by the steep turn of Sweetwater.

Let them alone, dear Aunt, just for one minute
Till I go fishing in the dark of my mind:
Where have I seen before, against the wind,
These bright virgins, robed and bare of bonnet,

Flowing with music of their strange quick tongue
And adventuring with delicate paces by the stream,—
Myself a child, old suddenly at the scream
From one of the white throats which it hid among?

CAPTAIN CARPENTER

Captain Carpenter rose up in his prime
Put on his pistols and went riding out
But had got well-nigh nowhere at that time
Till he fell in with ladies in a rout.

It was a pretty lady and all her train
That played with him so sweetly but before

An hour she'd taken a sword with all her main
And twined him of his nose for evermore.

Captain Carpenter mounted up one day
And rode straightway into a stranger rogue
That looked unchristian but be that as may
The Captain did not wait upon prologue.

But drew upon him out of his great heart
The other swung against him with a club
And cracked his two legs at the shinny part
And let him roll and stick like any tub.

Captain Carpenter rode many a time
From male and female took he sundry harms
He met the wife of Satan crying 'I'm
The she-wolf bids you shall bear no more arms'.

Their strokes and counters whistled in the wind
I wish he had delivered half his blows
But where she should have made off like a hind
The bitch bit off his arms at the elbows.

And Captain Carpenter parted with his ears
To a black devil that used him in this wise
O Jesus ere his threescore and ten years
Another had plucked out his sweet blue eyes.

Captain Carpenter got up on his roan
And sallied from the gate in hell's despite
I heard him asking in the grimmest tone
If any enemy yet there was to fight?

'To any adversary it is fame
If he risk to be wounded by my tongue
Or burnt in two beneath my red heart's flame
Such are the perils he is cast among.

187

JOHN
CROWE
RANSOM

'But if he can he has a pretty choice
From an anatomy with little to lose
Whether he cut my tongue and take my voice
Or whether it be my round red heart he choose.'

It was the neatest knave that ever was seen
Stepping in perfume from his lady's bower
Who at this word put in his merry mien
And fell on Captain Carpenter like a tower.

I would not knock old fellows in the dust
But there lay Captain Carpenter on his back
His weapons were the old heart in his bust
And a blade shook between rotten teeth alack.

The rogue in scarlet and gray soon knew his mind
He wished to get his trophy and depart
With gentle apology and touch refined
He pierced him and produced the Captain's heart.

God's mercy rest on Captain Carpenter now
I thought him Sirs an honest gentleman
Citizen husband soldier and scholar enow
Let jangling kites eat of him if they can.

But God's deep curses follow after those
That shore him of his goodly nose and ears
His legs and strong arms at the two elbows
And eyes that had not watered seventy years.

The curse of hell upon the sleek upstart
Who got the Captain finally on his back
And took the red red vitals of his heart
And made the kites to whet their beaks clack clack.

DEAD BOY

JOHN
CROWE
RANSOM

The little cousin is dead, by foul subtraction,
A green bough from Virginia's aged tree,
And neither the county kin love the transaction
Nor some of the world of outer dark, like me.

He was not a beautiful boy, nor good, nor clever,
A black cloud full of storms too hot for keeping,
A sword beneath his mother's heart,—yet never
Woman bewept her babe as this is weeping.

A pig with a pasty face, I had always said.
Squealing for cookies, kinned by pure pretence
With a noble house. But the little man quite dead,
I can see the forebears' antique lineaments.

The elder men have strode by the box of death
To the wide flag porch, and muttering low send round
The bruit of the day. O friendly waste of breath!
Their hearts are hurt with a deep dynastic wound.

He was pale and little, the foolish neighbors say;
The first-fruits, saith the preacher, the Lord hath
        taken;
But this was the old tree's late branch wrenched away,
Aggrieving the sapless limbs, the shorn and shaken.

JOHN
CROWE
RANSOM

Beautiful as the flying legend of some leopard,
She had not yet chosen her great captain or prince
Depositary to her flesh, and our defence;
And a wandering beauty is a blade out of its scabbard.
You know how dangerous, gentlemen of three-score?
May you know it yet ten more.

Nor by process of veiling she grew the less fabulous.
Gray or blue veils, we were desperate to study
The invincible emanations of her white body,
And the winds at her ordered raiment were ominous.
Might she walk in the market, sit in the council of
    soldiers?
Only of the extreme elders.

But a rare chance was the girl's then, when the
    Invader
Trumpeted from the south, and rumbled from the
    north,
Beleaguered the city from four quarters of the earth,
Our soldiery too craven and sick to aid her—
Where were the arms could countervail his horde?
Her beauty was the sword.

She sat with the elders, and proved on their blear
    visage
How bright was the weapon unrusted in her keeping,
While he lay surfeiting on their harvest heaping,
Wasting the husbandry of their rarest vintage—
And dreaming of the broad-breasted dames for
    concubine?
These floated on his wine.

He was lapped with bay-leaves, and grass and fumiter
    weed,
And from under the wine-film encountered his mortal
    vision.
For even within his tent she accomplished his derision;
She loosed one veil and another, standing unafraid;
And he perished. Nor brushed her with even so much
    as a daisy?
She found his destruction easy.

The heathen are all perished. The victory was
    furnished,
We smote them hiding in our vineyards, barns,
    annexes,
And now their white bones clutter the holes of foxes,
And the chieftain's head, with grinning sockets, and
    varnished—
Is it hung on the sky with a hideous epitaphy?
No, the woman keeps the trophy.

May God send unto the virtuous lady her prince.
It is stated she went reluctant to that orgy,
Yet a madness fevers our young men, and not the
    clergy
Nor the elders have turned them unto modesty since.
Inflamed by the thought of her naked beauty with
    desire?
Yes, and chilled with fear and despair.

JOHN
CROWE
RANSOM

ALLEN TATE

HORATIAN EPODE
TO THE DUCHESS OF MALFI

DUCHESS: *'Who am I?'*
BOSOLA: *'Thou art a box of worm-seed, at best but a*
salvatory of green mummy.'

The stage is about to be swept of corpses.
You have no more chance than an infusorian
Lodged in a hollow molar of an eohippus.
Come, now, no prattle of remergence with the
  ὄντως ὄν.

. . . .

As (the form requires the myth)
A Greek girl stood once in the prytaneum
Of Carneades, hearing mouthings of Probability,
Then mindful of love dashed her brain on a megalith,

So you, O nameless Duchess who die young,
Meet death somewhat lovingly
And I am filled with a pity of beholding skulls.
There was no pride like yours.

Now considerations of the Void coming after,
Not changed by the strict gesture of your death,
Split the straight line of pessimism
Into two infinities.

It is moot whether there be divinities
As I finish this play by Webster:
The street cars are still running however
And the katharsis fades in the warm water of a yawn.

1922

IDIOT

ALLEN
TATE

The idiot greens the meadow with his eyes,
The meadow creeps, implacable and still;
A dog barks; the hammock swings; he lies.
One, two, three, the cows bulge on the hill.

Motion, which is not time, erects snowdrifts
While sister's hand sieves waterfalls of lace.
With a palm fan closer than death, he lifts
The Ozarks and tilted seas across his face.

In the long sunset where impatient sound
Strips niggers to a multiple of backs,
Flies yield their heat, magnolias drench the ground
With Appomattox! The shadows lie in stacks.

The julep glass weaves echoes in Jim's kinks
While ashy Jim puts murmurs in the day:
Now in the idiot's heart a chamber stinks
Of dead asters—as the potter's field, of May.

All evening the marsh is a slick pool
Where dream wild hares, witch hazel, pretty girls.
'Up from the important picnic of a fool
Those rotted asters!' Eddy on eddy swirls

The innocent mansion of a panther's heart!
It crumbles; tick-tick, time drags it in;
And now his arteries lag and now they start
Reverence with the frigid gusts of sin.

The stillness pelts the eye, assaults the hair;
A beech sticks out a branch to warn the stars;

A lightning-bug jerks angles in the air,
Diving, 'I am the captain of new wars!'

The dusk runs down the lane, driven like hail;
Far-off a precise whistle is escheat
To the dark; and then the towering weak and pale
Covers his eyes with memory like a sheet.

1926

THE MEDITERRANEAN

Quem das finem, rex magne, dolorum?

Where we went in the boat was a long bay
A slingshot wide walled in by towering stone,
Peaked margin of antiquity's delay—
And we went there out of time's monotone:

Where we went in the black hull no light moved
But a gull white-winged along the feckless wave;
The breeze, unseen but fierce as a body loved,
That boat drove onward like a willing slave;

Where we went in the small ship the seaweed
Parted and gave to us the murmuring shore
And we made feast and in our secret need
Devoured the very plates Aeneas bore:

Where derelict you see through the low twilight
The green coast that you thunder-tossed would win
Drop sail, and hastening to drink all night
Eat dish and bowl—to take the sweet land in!

Where we feasted and caroused on the sandless
Pebbles, affecting our day of piracy,

What prophecy of eaten plates could landless
Wanderers fulfil by the ancient sea?

ALLEN
TATE

We for that time might taste the famous age
Eternal here yet hidden from our eyes
When lust of power undid its stuffless rage;
They, in a wineskin, bore earth's paradise.

—Let us lie down once more by the breathing side
Of ocean, where our live forefathers sleep
As if the Known Sea still were a month wide—
Atlantis howls but is no longer steep!

What country shall we conquer, what fair land
Unman our conquest and locate our blood?
We've cracked the hemispheres with careless hand:
Now, from the Gates of Hercules we flood

Westward, westward till the barbarous brine
Whelms us to the tired world where tasseling corn,
Fat beans, grapes sweeter than muscadine
Rot on the vine: in that land were we born.

1932

THE OATH

It was near evening, the room was cold,
Half-dark; Uncle Ben's brass bullet-mould
And powder horn, and Major Bogan's face
Above the fire, in the half-light, plainly said
There's naught to kill but the animated dead;
Horn nor mould nor Major follows the chase.
Being cold I urged Lytle to the fire
In the blank twilight, with not much left untold
By two old friends when neither's a great liar;
We sat down evenly in the smoky chill.
There's precious little to say betwixt day and dark,
Perhaps a few words on the implacable will
Of time sailing like a magic barque
Or something as fine for the amenities,
Till the dusk seals the window, the fire grows bright
And the wind saws the hill with a swarm of bees.
Now meditating a little on the firelight
We heard the darkness grapple with the night
And give an old man's valedictory wheeze
From his westward breast between his polar jaws;
So Lytle asked: Who are the dead?
Who are the living and the dead? . . .
And nothing more was said;
But I leaving Lytle to that dream
Decided what it is in time that gnaws
The aging fury of a mountain stream,
When suddenly as an ignorant mind will do
I thought I heard the dark pounding its head
On a rock, crying *Who are the dead?*
Lytle turned with an oath—By God, it's true!

1930

ODE TO THE CONFEDERATE DEAD

ALLEN
TATE

Row after row with strict impunity
The headstones yield their names to the element,
The wind whirrs without recollection;
In the riven troughs the splayed leaves
Pile up, of nature the casual sacrament
To the seasonal eternity of death,
Then driven by the fierce scrutiny
Of heaven to their business in the vast breath,
They sough the rumour of mortality.

Autumn is desolation in the plot
Of a thousand acres, where these memories grow
From the inexhaustible bodies that are not
Dead, but feed the grass row after rich row:
Remember now the autumns that have gone—
Ambitious November with the humors of the year,
With a particular zeal for every slab,
Staining the uncomfortable angels that rot
On the slabs, a wing chipped here, an arm there:
The brute curiosity of an angel's stare
Turns you like them to stone,
Transforms the heaving air,
Till plunged to a heavier world below
You shift your sea-space blindly,
Heaving, turning like the blind crab.

      Dazed by the wind, only the wind
      The leaves flying, plunge

You know who have waited by the wall
The twilit certainty of an animal;
Those midnight restitutions of the blood
You know—the immitigable pines, the smoky frieze

ALLEN Of the sky, the sudden call; you know the rage—
TATE   The cold pool left by the mounting flood—
The rage of Zeno and Parmenides.
You who have waited for the angry resolution
Of those desires that should be yours tomorrow,
You know the unimportant shrift of death
And praise the vision
And praise the arrogant circumstance
Of those who fall
Rank upon rank, hurried beyond decision—
Here by the sagging gate, stopped by the wall.

       Seeing, seeing only the leaves
       Flying, plunge and expire

Turn your eyes to the immoderate past
Turn to the inscrutable infantry rising
Demons out of the earth—they will not last.
Stonewall, Stonewall—and the sunken fields of hemp
Shiloh, Antietam, Malvern Hill, Bull Run.
Lost in that orient of the thick and fast
You will curse the setting sun.

       Cursing only the leaves crying
       Like an old man in a storm

You hear the shout—the crazy hemlocks point
With troubled fingers to the silence which
Smothers you, a mummy, in time. The hound bitch
Toothless and dying, in a musty cellar
Hears the wind only.

           Now that the salt of their blood
Stiffens the saltier oblivion of the sea,
Seals the malignant purity of the flood,
What shall we, who count our days and bow

Our heads with a commemorial woe,
In the ribboned coats of grim felicity,
What shall we say of the bones, unclean—
Their verdurous anonymity will grow—
The ragged arms, the ragged heads and eyes
Lost in these acres of the insane green?
The grey lean spiders come; they come and go;
In a tangle of willows without light
The singular screech-owl's bright
Invisible lyric seeds the mind
With the furious murmur of their chivalry.

          We shall say only, the leaves
             Flying, plunge and expire

We shall say only, the leaves whispering
In the improbable mist of nightfall
That flies on multiple wing:
Night is the beginning and the end,
And in between the ends of distraction
Waits mute speculation, the patient curse
That stones the eyes, or like the jaguar leaps
For his own image in a jungle pool, his victim.

What shall we say who have knowledge
Carried to the heart? Shall we take the act
To the grave? Shall we, more hopeful, set up the grave
In the house? The ravenous grave?

                          Leave now
The turnstile and the old stone wall:
The gentle serpent, green in the mulberry bush,
Riots with his tongue through the hush—
Sentinel of the grave who counts us all!

1926-1930

HART CRANE

NORTH LABRADOR

A land of leaning ice
Hugged by plaster-grey arches of sky,
Flings itself silently
Into eternity.

'Has no one come here to win you,
Or left you with the faintest blush
Upon your glittering breasts?
Have you no memories, O Darkly Bright?'

Cold-hushed, there is only the shifting of moments
That journey toward no Spring—
No birth, no death, no time nor sun
In answer.

RECITATIVE

Regard the capture here, O Janus-faced,
As double as the hands that twist this glass.
Such eyes at search or rest you cannot see;
Reciting pain or glee, how can you bear!

Twin shadowed halves: the breaking second holds
In each the skin alone, and so it is
I crust a plate of vibrant mercury
Borne cleft to you, and brother in the half.

Inquire this much-exacting fragment smile,
Its drums and darkest blowing leaves ignore,—

Defer though, revocation of the tears
That yield attendance to one crucial sign.

Look steadily—how the wind feasts and spins
The brain's disk shivered against lust. Then watch
While darkness, like an ape's face, falls away,
And gradually white buildings answer day.

Let the same nameless gulf beleaguer us—
Alike suspend us from atrocious sums
Built floor by floor on shafts of steel that grant
The plummet heart, like Absalom, no stream.

The highest tower,—let her ribs palisade
Wrenched gold of Nineveh;—yet leave the tower.
The bridge swings over salvage, beyond wharves;
A wind abides the ensign of your will . . .

In alternating bells have you not heard
All hours clapped dense into a single stride?
Forgive me for an echo of these things,
And let us walk through time with equal pride.

FOR THE MARRIAGE OF FAUSTUS
AND HELEN

III

Capped arbiter of beauty in this street
That narrows darkly into motor dawn,—
You, here beside me, delicate ambassador
Of intricate slain numbers that arise
In whispers, naked of steel;

       religious gunman!
Who faithfully, yourself, will fall too soon,
And in other ways than as the wind settles

HART On the sixteen thrifty bridges of the city:
CRANE Let us unbind our throats of fear and pity.

We even,
Who drove speediest destruction
In corymbulous formations of mechanics,—
Who hurried the hill breezes, spouting malice
Plangent over meadows, and looked down
On rifts of torn and empty houses
Like old women with teeth unjubilant
That waited faintly, briefly and in vain:

We know, eternal gunman, our flesh remembers
The tensile boughs, the nimble blue plateaus,
The mounted, yielding cities of the air!
That saddled sky that shook down vertical
Repeated play of fire—no hypogeum
Of wave or rock was good against one hour.
We did not ask for that, but have survived,
And will persist to speak again before
All stubble streets that have not curved
To memory, or known the ominous lifted arm
That lowers down the arc of Helen's brow
To saturate with blessing and dismay.

A goose, tobacco and cologne—
Three winged and gold-shod prophecies of heaven,
The lavish heart shall always have to leaven
And spread with bells and voices, and atone
The abating shadows of our conscript dust.

Anchises' navel, dripping of the sea,—
The hands Erasmus dipped in gleaming tides,
Gathered the voltage of blown blood and vine;
Delve upward for the new and scattered wine,

O brother-thief of time, that we recall.
Laugh out the meagre penance of their days
Who dare not share with us the breath released,
The substance drilled and spent beyond repair
For golden, or the shadow of gold hair.
Distinctly praise the years, whose volatile
Blamed bleeding hands extend and thresh the height
The imagination spans beyond despair,
Outpacing bargain, vocable and prayer.

CUTTY SARK

> *O, the navies old and oaken*
> *O, the Temeraire no more!*
>
> MELVILLE

I met a man in South Street, tall—
a nervous shark tooth swung on his chain.
His eyes pressed through green grass
—green glasses, or bar lights made them
so—

      shine—
         GREEN—
               eyes—
stepped out—forgot to look at you
or left you several blocks away—

in the nickel-in-the-slot piano jogged
'Stamboul Nights'—weaving somebody's nickel—
    sang—

      O Stamboul Rose—dreams weave the rose!

       Murmurs of Leviathan he spoke,
       and rum was Plato in our heads . . .

HART **'It's** S.S. *Ala*—Antwerp—now remember kid
CRANE to put me out at three she sails on time.
    I'm not much good at time any more keep
    weakeyed watches sometimes snooze—' his bony hands
    got to beating time . . . 'A whaler once—
    I ought to keep time and get over it—I'm a
    Democrat—I know what time it is—No
    I don't want to know what time it is—that
    damned white Arctic killed my time . . .'

        O Stamboul Rose—drums weave—

    'I ran a donkey engine down there on the Canal
    in Panama—got tired of that—
    then Yucatan selling kitchenware—beads—
    have you seen Popocatepetl—birdless mouth
    with ashes sifting down—?
                    and then the coast again . . .'

        Rose of Stamboul O coral Queen—
        teased remnants of the skeletons of cities—
        and galleries, galleries of watergutted lava
        snarling stone—green—drums—drown—

Sing!
'—that spiracle!' he shot a finger out the door . . .
'O life's a geyser—beautiful—my lungs—
No—I can't live on land—!'

I saw the frontiers gleaming of his mind;
or are there frontiers—running sands sometimes
running sands—somewhere—sands running . . .
Or they may start some white machine that sings.
Then you may laugh and dance the axletree—
steel—silver—kick the traces—and know—

ATLANTIS ROSE drums wreathe the rose,
the star floats burning in a gulf of tears
and sleep another thousand—

                        interminably

long since somebody's nickel—stopped—
playing—

A wind worried those wicker-neat lapels, the
swinging summer entrances to cooler hells . . .
Outside a wharf truck nearly ran him down
—he lunged up Bowery way while the dawn
was putting the Statue of Liberty out—that
torch of hers you know—

I started walking home across the Bridge . . .

    .   .   .   .

Blithe Yankee vanities, turreted sprites, winged
                     British repartees, skil-
ful savage sea-girls
that bloomed in the spring—Heave, weave
those bright designs the trade winds drive . . .

       Sweet opium and tea, Yo-ho!
      Pennies for porpoises that bank the keel!
      Fins whip the breeze around Japan!

Bright skysails ticketing the Line, wink round the
     Horn
to Frisco, Melbourne . . .
                      Pennants, parabolas—
clipper dreams indelible and ranging,
baronial white on lucky blue!

     Perennial-*Cutty*-trophied-*Sark*!

HART *Thermopylæ, Black Prince, Flying Cloud* through Sunda
CRANE —scarfed of foam, their bellies veered green
       esplanades,
    locked in wind-humors, ran their eastings down;

          at Java Head freshened the nip
          (sweet opium and tea!)
          and turned and left us on the lee . . .

Buntlines tusselling (91 days, 20 hours and anchored!)
                     Rainbow, Leander
(last trip a tragedy)—where can you be
Nimbus? and you rivals two—

        a long tack keeping—

                Taeping?
                Ariel?

E. E. CUMMINGS

ONE X

death is more than
certain a hundred these
sounds crowds odours it
is in a hurry
beyond that any this
taxi smile or angle we do

not sell and buy
things so necessary as
is death and unlike shirts
neckties trousers
we cannot wear it out

no sir which is why
granted who discovered
America ether the movies
may claim general importance

to me to you nothing is
what particularly
matters hence in a

little sunlight and less
moonlight ourselves against the worms

hate laugh shimmy

16 heures
l'Etoile

the communists have fine Eyes

some are young some old none
look alike the flics rush
batter the crowd sprawls collapses
singing knocked down trampled the kicked by
flics rush (the

Flics, tidiyum, are
very tidiyum reassuringly similar,
they all have very tidiyum
mustaches, and very
tidiyum chins, and just above
their very tidiyum ears their
very tidiyum necks begin)
                              let us add

that there are 50 (fifty) flics for every
one (1) communist and
all the flics are very organically
arranged
and their nucleus (composed
of captains in freshly-creased
-uniforms with only-just-
shined buttons
tidiyum
before and behind) has a nucleolus:

the Prefect of Police

(a dapper derbied
creature, swaggers daintily

twiddling
his tiny cane
and mazurkas about tweak-
ing his wing collar pecking at his im

-peccable cravat directing being
shooting his cuffs
saluted everywhere saluting
reviewing processions of minions
tappingpeopleontheback

'allezcirculez')

—my   he's brave . . .
the
communists pick
up themselves friends
& their hats legs &

arms brush dirt coats
smile looking hands
spit blood teeth

the Communists have (very) fine eyes
(which stroll hither and thither through the
evening in bruised narrow questioning faces)

here's a little mouse) and
what does he think about, i
wonder as over this
floor (quietly with

bright eyes) drifts (nobody
can tell because
Nobody knows, or why
jerks Here &, here,
gr(oo)ving the room's Silence) this like
a littlest
poem a
(with wee ears and see?

tail frisks)
            (gonE)
'mouse',
            We are not the same you and

i, since here's a little he
or is
it It
? (or was something we saw in the mirror)?

therefore we'll kiss; for maybe
what was Disappeared
into ourselves
who (look). ,startled

LAURA RIDING

THE TILLAQUILS

Dancing lamely on a lacquered plain,
Never a Tillaquil murmurs for legs.
Embrace rustles a windy wistfulness,
But feels for no hands.
Scant stir of being, yet rather they
Unfulfilled unborn than failing alive,
Escaping the public shame of history.

Once only two Tillaquils nearly a man and woman
Violated a hopeless code with hope,
Slept a single dream seeming in time.
'Come,' he cried, coaxing her,
'Stairs stream upward not for rest at every step
But to reach the top always before Death.'
'Softly,' she whispered,
'Or two Tillaquils will wake.'

Death they passed always over and over,
Life grew always sooner and sooner.
But love like a grimace
Too real on Life's face
Smiled two terrified dreams of Tillaquils
Tremblingly down the falling flights;
Who saved themselves in waking
The waste of being something.
And danced traditionally
To nothingness and never;
With only a lost memory
Punishing this foolish pair
That nearly lived and loved
In one nightmare.

LUCRECE AND NARA

Astonished stood Lucrece and Nara,
Face flat to face, one sense and smoothness.
'Love, is this face or flesh,
Love, is this you?'
One breath drew the dear lips close and whispered,
'Nara, is there a miracle can last?'
'Lucrece, is there a simple thing can stay?'

Unnoticed as a single raindrop
Broke each dawn until
Blindness as the same day fell.
'How is the opalescence of my white hand, Nara?
Is it still pearly cool?'
'How is the faintness of my neck, Lucrece?
Is it blood shy with warmth, as always?'

Ghostly they clung and questioned
A thousand years, not yet eternal,
True to their fading,
Through their long watch defying
Time to make them whole, to part them.

A gentle clasp and fragrance played and hung
A thousand years and more
Around earth closely.
'Earth will be long enough,
Love has no elsewhere.'

And when earth ended, was devoured
One shivering midsummer
At the dissolving border,
A sound of light was felt.
'Nara, is it you, the dark?'
'Lucrece, is it you, the quiet?'

THE MAP OF PLACES

LAURA
RIDING

The map of places passes.
The reality of paper tears.
Land and water where they are
Are only where they were
When words read *here* and *here*
Before ships happened there.

Now on naked names feet stand,
No geographies in the hand,
And paper reads anciently,
And ships at sea
Turn round and round.
All is known, all is found.
Death meets itself everywhere.
Holes in maps look through to nowhere.

THE TIGER

The tiger in me I know late, not burning bright.
Of such women as I am, they say,
'Woman, many women in one,' winking.
Such women as I say, thinking,
'A procession of one, reiteration
Of blinking eyes and disentangled brains
Measuring their length in love.
A yard of thought marks the embrace.
To these I have charms.
Shame, century creature.'
To myself, hurrying, I whisper,
'The lechery of time greases their eyes.

Lust, earlier than time,
Unwinds their mind.
The green anatomy of desire
Plain as through glass
Quickens as I pass.'

Earlier than lust, not plain,
Behind a darkened face of memory,
My inner animal revives.
Beware, that I am tame.
Beware philosophies
Wherein I yield.

They cage me on three sides.
The fourth is glass.
Not to be image of the beast in me,
I press the tiger forward.
I crash through.
Now we are two.
One rides.

And now I know the tiger late,
And now they pursue:
'A woman in a skin, mad at her heels
With pride, pretending chariot wheels.
Fleeing our learned days,
She reassumes the brute.'

The first of the pursuers found me.
With lady-ears I listened.
'Dear face, to find you here
After such tiger-hunt and pressing of
Thick forest, to find you here
In high house in a jungle,
To brave as any room
The tiger-cave and as in any room

Find woman in the room
With dear face shaking her dress
To wave like any picture queen . . .'
'Dear pursuer, to find me thus
Belies no tiger. The tiger runs and rides,
But the lady is not venturous.

LAURA
RIDING

'Like any picture queen she hides
And is unhappy in her room,
Covering her eyes against the latest year,
Its learning of old queens,
Its death to queens and pictures,
Its lust of century creatures,
And century creatures as one woman,
Such a woman as I,
Mirage of all green forests—
The colour of the season always
When hope lives of abolished pleasures.'

So to the first pursuer I prolonged
Woman's histories and shames,
And yielded as became a queen
Picture-dreaming in a room
Among silk provinces where pain
Ruined her body without stain—
So white, so out of time, so story-like.
While woman's pride escaped
In tiger stripes.

Hymn to the hostage queen
And her debauched provinces.
Down fell her room,
Down fell her high couches.
The first pursuer rose from his hot cloak.
'Company,' he cried, 'the tiger made magic

While you slept and I dreamt of ravages.
The queen was dust.'
And Queen, Queen, Queen
Crowded the Captain's brain.
And Queen, Queen, Queen
Spurred the whole train
With book-thoughts
And exploits of queen's armies
On gold and silver cloth.
Until they stumbled on their eyes,
Read the number of the year,
Remembered the fast tiger.

The tiger recalled man's fear
Of beast, in man-sweat they ran back,
Opened their books to the correct pages.
The chapter closed with queens and shepherdesses.
'Peace to their dim tresses,'
Chanted the pious sages.

And now the tiger in me I knew late.
'O pride,' I comforted, 'rest.
The mischief and the rape
Cannot come through.
We are in the time of never yet
Where bells peal backward,
Peal ''forget, forget''.'

Here am I found forgotten.
The sun is used. The men are in the book.
I, woman, have removed the window
And read in my high house in the dark,
Sitting long after reading, as before,
Waiting, as in the book, to hear the bell,
Though long since has fallen away the door,

Long since, when like a tiger I was pursued

And the first pursuer, at such and such a date,
Found how the tiger takes the lady
Far away where she is gentle.
In the high forest she is gentle.
She is patient in a high house.
Ah me, Ah me, says every lady in the end,
Putting the tiger in its cage
Inside her lofty head.
And weeps reading her own story.
And scarcely knows she weeps,
So loud the tiger roars.
Or thinks to close her eyes,
Though surely she must be sleeping,
To go on without knowing weeping,
Sleeping or not knowing,
Not knowing weeping,
Not knowing sleeping.

THE WIND, THE CLOCK, THE WE

The wind has at last got into the clock—
Every minute for itself.
There's no more sixty,
There's no more twelve,
It's as late as it's early.

The rain has washed out the numbers.
The trees don't care what happens.
Time has become a landscape
Of suicidal leaves and stoic branches—
Unpainted as fast as painted.

Or perhaps that's too much to say,
With the clock swimming in itself
And the minutes given leave to die.

The sea's no picture at all.
To sea, then: that's time now,
And every mortal heart's a sailor
Sworn to vengeance on the wind,
To hurl life back into the thin teeth
Out of which first it whistled,
An idiotic defiance of it knew not what
Screeching round the studying clock.

Now there's neither ticking nor blowing.
The ship has gone down with its men,
The sea with the ship, the wind with the sea.
The wind at last got into the clock,
The clock at last got into the wind,
The world at last got out of itself.
At last we can make sense, you and I,
You lone survivor on paper,
The wind's boldness and the clock's care
Become a voiceless language,
And I the story hushed in it—
Is more to say of me?
Do I say more than self-choked hesitation
Can repeat word for word after me,
The script not altered by a breath
Of perhaps meaning otherwise?

THE WIND SUFFERS

LAURA
RIDING

The wind suffers of blowing,
The sea suffers of water,
And fire suffers of burning,
And I of a living name.

As stone suffers of stoniness,
As light of its shiningness,
As birds of their wingedness,
So I of my whoness.

And what the cure of all this?
What the not and not suffering?
What the better and later of this?
What the more me of me?

How for the pain-world to be
More world and no pain?
How for the faithful rain to fall
More wet and more dry?

How for the wilful blood to run
More salt-red and sweet-white?
And how for me in my actualness
To more shriek and more smile?

By no other miracles,
By the same knowing poison,
By an improved anguish,
By my further dying.

THE FLOWERING URN

And every prodigal greatness
Must creep back into strange home,
Must fill the empty matrix of
The never-begotten perfect son
Who never can be born.

And every quavering littleness
Must pale more tinily than it knows
Into the giant hush whose sound
Reverberates within itself
As tenderest numbers cannot improve.

And from this jealous secrecy
Will rise itself, will flower up
The likeness kept against false seed:
When death-whole is the seed
And no new harvest will fraction sowing.

Will rise the same peace that held
Before fertility's lie awoke
The virgin sleep of Mother All:
The same but for the way in flowering
It speaks of fruits that could not be

NOR IS IT WRITTEN

LAURA
RIDING

Nor is it written that you may not grieve.
There is no rule of joy, long may you dwell
Not smiling yet in that last pain,
On that last supper of the heart's palate.
It is not written that you must take joy
In that not thus again shall you sit down
To spread that mingled banquet
Which the deep larder of illusion spilled
Like ancient riches in time grown not astonishing.
Lean to the cloth awhile, and yet awhile,
And even may your eyes caress
Proudly the used abundance.
It is not written in what heart
You may not pass from ancient plenty
Into the straitened nowadays.
To each is given secrecy of heart,
To make himself what heart he please
In stirring up from that fond table
To sit him down at this sharp meal.
It shall not here be asked of him
'What thinks your heart?'
Long may you sorely to yourself accuse
This single bread and truth,
This disenchanted understanding.
It is not counted what loud passions
Your heart in ancient private keeps alive.
To each is given what defeat he will.

AUSPICE OF JEWELS

They have connived at those jewelled fascinations
That to our hands and arms and ears
And heads and necks and feet
And all the winding stalk
Extended the mute spell of the face.

They have endowed the whole of us
With such a solemn gleaming
As in the dark of flesh-love
But the face at first did have.
We are studded with wide brilliance
As the world with towns and cities—
The travelling look builds capitals
Where the evasive eye may rest
Safe from the too immediate lodgement.

Obscure and bright these forms
Which as the women of their lingering thought
In slow translucence we have worn.
And the silent given glitter locks us
In a not false unplainness:
Have we ourselves been sure
What steady countenance to turn them?

Until now—when this passionate neglect
Of theirs, and our twinkling reluctance,
Are like the reader and the book
Whose fingers and whose pages have confided
But whose sight and sense
Meet in a chilly time of strangeness;

And it is once more early, anxious,
And so late, it is intolerably the same
Not speaking coruscation

That both we and they made endless, dream-long, LAURA
Lest be cruel to so much love RIDING
The closer shine of waking,
And what be said sound colder
Than the ghastly love-lisp.

Until now—when to go jewelled
We must despoil the drowsy masquerade
Where gloom of silk and gold
And glossy dazed adornments
Kept safe from flagrant realness
The forgeries of ourselves we were—
When to be alive as love feigned us
We must steal death and its wan splendours
From the women of their sighs we were.

For we are now otherwise luminous.
The light which was spent in jewels
Has performed upon the face
A gradual eclipse of recognition.
We have passed from plaintive visibility
Into total rareness,
And from this reunion of ourselves and them
Under the snuffed lantern of time
Comes an astonished flash like truth
Or the unseen-unheard entrance of someone
Whom eyes and ears in their dotage
Have forgotten for dead or lost.

(And hurrying toward distracted glory,
Gemmed lady-pageants, bells on their hearts,
By restless knights attended
Whose maudlin plumes and pommels
Urge the adventure past return.)

ROBERT GRAVES

QUAYSIDE

And glad to find, on again looking at it,
It was not nearly so good as I had thought—
You know the ship is moving when you see
The boxes on the quayside sliding away
And growing smaller—and having real delight
When the port's cleared and the coast out of sight,
And ships are few, each on its proper course,
With no occasion for approach or discourse.

O LOVE IN ME

O love, be fed with apples while you may,
And feel the sun and go in royal array,
A smiling innocent on the heavenly causeway.

Though in what listening horror for the cry
That soars in outer blackness dismally,
The dumb blind beast, the paranoiac fury,

Be warm, enjoy the season, lift your head,
Exquisite in the pulse of tainted blood,
That shivering glory not to be despised.

Take your delight in momentariness,
Walk between dark and dark, a shining space
With the grave's narrowness, though not its peace.

INTERRUPTION

ROBERT
GRAVES

If ever against this easy blue and silver
Hazed-over countryside of thoughtfulness
Far behind in the mind and above,
Boots from before and below approach tramping,
Watch how their premonition will display
A forward countryside, low in the distance,
A picture-postcard square of June grass,
Will warm a summer season, trim the hedges,
Cast the river about on either flank,
Start the late cuckoo emptily calling,
Invent a rambling tale of moles and voles,
Furnish a path with stiles.
Watch how the field will broaden, the feet nearing,
Sprout with great dandelions and buttercups,
Widen and heighten. The blue and silver
Fogs at the border of this all-grass.
Interruption looms gigantified,
Lurches against, treads thundering through,
Blots the landscape, scatters all,
Roars and rumbles like a dark tunnel,
Is gone.

The picture-postcard grass and trees
Swim back to central: it is a large patch,
It is a modest, failing patch of green,
The postage-stamp of its departure,
Clouded with blue and silver, closing in now
To a plain countryside of less and less,
Unpeopled and unfeatured blue and silver,
Before, behind, above.

LOST ACRES

These acres, always again lost
　　By every new Ordnance-survey
And searched for at exhausting cost
　　Of time and thought, are still away.

They have their paper-substitute—
　　Intercalation of an inch
At the so many thousandth foot:
　　And no one parish feels the pinch.

But lost they are, despite all care,
　　So perhaps likeliest to be bound
Together in a piece somewhere,
　　A plot of undiscovered ground.

Invisible, they have the spite
　　To swerve the tautest measuring chain
And the exact theodolite
　　Perched every side of them in vain.

Yet there's no scientific need
　　To plot these acres of the mind
With prehistoric fern and reed
　　And monsters such as heroes find.

They have, no doubt, their flowers, their birds,
　　Their trees behind the phantom fence,
But of the substance of mere words:
　　To walk there would be loss of sense.

THE BARDS

heir cheeks are blotched for shame, their running
    verse
tumbles, with marrow-bones the drunken diners
elt them as they delay:
 is a something fearful in the song
lagues them, an unknown grief that like a churl
oes commonplace in cowskin
nd bursts unheralded, crowing and coughing,
n unpilled holly-club twirled in his hand,
ito their many-shielded, samite-curtained
ewel-bright hall where twelve kings sit at chess
Over the white-bronze pieces and the gold,
nd by a gross enchantment
lails down the rafters and leads off the queens—
he wild-swan-breasted, the rose-ruddy-cheeked
aven-haired daughters of their admiration—
o stir his black pots and to bed on straw

FLYING CROOKED

The butterfly, the cabbage-white,
(His honest idiocy of flight)
Will never now, it is too late,
Master the art of flying straight,
Yet has—who knows so well as I?—
A just sense of how not to fly:
He lurches here and here by guess
And God and hope and hopelessness.
Even the aerobatic swift
Has not his flying-crooked gift.

TIME

The vague sea thuds against the marble cliffs
And from their fragments age-long grinds
Pebbles like flowers.

Or the vague weather wanders in the fields,
When up spring flowers with coloured buds
Like marble pebbles.

The beauty of the flowers is Time, death-grieved:
The pebbles' beauty too is Time,
Life-weary.

It is all too easy to admire a flower
Or a smooth pebble flower-like freaked
By Time and vagueness.

Time is Time's ease and the sweet oil that coaxes
All obstinate locks and rusty hinges
To loving-kindness.

What monster's proof against that lovesome pair,
Old age and childhood, seals of Time,
His sorrowful vagueness?

Or will not render him the accustomed thanks,
Humouring age with filial flowers,
Childhood with pebbles?

OGRES AND PYGMIES

Those famous men of old, the Ogres—
They had long beards and stinking arm-pits.
They were wide-mouthed, long-yarded and great-
    bellied

Yet of not taller stature, Sirs, than you.
They lived on Ogre-Strand, which was no place
But the churl's terror of their proud extent,
Where every foot was three-and-thirty inches
And every penny bought a whole sheep.
Now of their company none survive, not one,
The times being, thank God, unfavourable
To all but nightmare memory of them.
Their images stand howling in the waste,
(The winds enforced against their wide mouths)
Whose granite haunches king and priest must yearly
Buss, and their cold knobbed knees.
So many feats they did to admiration:
With their enormous lips they sang louder
Than ten cathedral choirs, with their grand yards
Stormed the most rare and obstinate maidenheads,
With their strong-gutted and capacious bellies
Digested stones and glass like ostriches.
They dug great pits and heaped great cairns,
Deflected rivers, slew whole armies,
And hammered judgements for posterity—
For the sweet-cupid-lipped and tassel-yarded
Delicate-stomached dwellers
In Pygmy Alley, where with brooding on them
A foot is shrunk to seven inches
And twelve-pence will not buy a spare rib.
And who would choose between Ogres and Pygmies—
The thundering text, the snivelling commentary—
Reading between such covers he will likely
Prove his own disproportion and not laugh.

THE LEGS

There was this road,
And it led up-hill,
And it led down-hill,
And round and in and out.

And the traffic was legs,
Legs from the knees down,
Coming and going,
Never pausing.

And the gutters gurgled
With the rain's overflow,
And the sticks on the pavement
Blindly tapped and tapped.

What drew the legs along
Was the never-stopping,
And the senseless frightening
Fate of being legs.

Legs for the road,
The road for legs,
Resolutely nowhere
In both directions.

My legs at least
Were not in that rout,
On grass by the road-side
Entire I stood,

Watching the unstoppable
Legs go by
With never a stumble
Between step and step.

Though my smile was broad
The legs could not see,
Though my laugh was loud
The legs could not hear.

My head dizzied then:
I wondered suddenly,
Might I too be a walker
From the knees down?

Gently I touched my shins.
The doubt unchained them:
They had run in twenty puddles
Before I regained them.

ROBERT
GRAVES

ON DWELLING

Courtesies of good-morning and good-evening
From rustic lips fail as the town encroaches:
Soon nothing passes but the cold quick stare
Of eyes that see ghosts, yet too many for fear.

Here I too walk, silent myself, in wonder
At a town not mine though plainly coextensive
With mine, even in days coincident:
In mine I dwell, in theirs like them I haunt.

And the green country, should I turn again there?
My bumpkin neighbours loom even ghostlier:
Like trees they murmur or like blackbirds sing
Courtesies of good-morning and good-evening.

TO WHOM ELSE?

To whom else other than,
To whom else not of man
Yet in human state,
Standing neither in stead
Of self nor idle godhead,
Should I, man in man bounded,
Myself dedicate?

To whom else momently,
To whom else endlessly,
But to you, I?
To you who only,
To you who mercilessly,
To you who lovingly,
Plucked out the lie?

To whom else less acquaint,
To whom else without taint
Of death, death-true?
With great astonishment
Thankfully I consent
To my estrangement
From me in you.

ON PORTENTS

If strange things happen where she is,
So that men say that graves open
And the dead walk, or that futurity
Becomes a womb and the unborn are shed,
Such portents are not to be wondered at,
Being tourbillions in Time made
By the strong pulling of her bladed mind
Through that ever-reluctant element.

TO BRING THE DEAD TO LIFE

ROBERT
GRAVES

To bring the dead to life
Is no great magic.
Few are wholly dead:
Blow on a dead man's embers
And a live flame will start.

Let his forgotten griefs be now,
And now his withered hopes;
Subject your pen to his handwriting
Until it prove as natural
To sign his name as yours.

Limp as he limped,
Swear by the oaths he swore;
If he wore black, affect the same;
If he had gouty fingers,
Be yours gouty too.

Assemble tokens intimate of him—
A ring, a purse, a chair:
Around these elements then build
A home familiar to
The greedy revenant.

So grant him life, but reckon
That the grave which housed him
May not be empty now:
You in his spotted garments
Must yourself lie wrapped.

THE KING OF CHINA'S DAUGHTER

The King of China's daughter,
She never would love me
Though I hung my cap and bells upon
Her nutmeg tree.
For oranges and lemons,
The stars in bright blue air,
(I stole them long ago, my dear)
Were dangling there.
The Moon did give me silver pence,
The Sun did give me gold,
And both together softly blew
And made my porridge cold;
But the King of China's daughter
Pretended not to see
When I hung my cap and bells upon
Her nutmeg tree.

HORNPIPE

Sailors come
To the drum
Out of Babylon;
    Hobby-horses
Foam, the dumb
Sky rhinoceros-glum

Watched the courses of the breakers' rocking-horses
    and with Glaucis,
Lady Venus on the settee of the horsehair sea!

Where Lord Tennyson in laurels wrote a gloria free
In a borealic iceberg came Victoria; she
Knew Prince Albert's tall memorial took the colours
    of the floreal
And the borealic iceberg; floating on they see
New-arisen Madam Venus for whose sake from far
Came the fat and zebra'd emperor from Zanzibar
Where like golden bouquets lay far Asia, Africa, Cathay,
All laid before that shady lady by the fibroid Shah.
Captain Fracasse stout as any water-butt came, stood
With Sir Bacchus both a-drinking the black tarr'd
    grapes' blood
Plucked among the tartan leafage
By the furry wind whose grief age
Could not wither—like a squirrel with a gold star-nut.
Queen Victoria sitting shocked upon the rocking-horse
Of a wave said to the Laureate, 'This minx of course
Is as sharp as any lynx and blacker-deeper than the
    drinks and quite as
Hot as any hottentot, without remorse!

      For the minx,'
             Said she,
    'And the drinks,
             You can see

Are hot as any hottentot and not the goods for me!'

EDITH
SITWELL

When
Sir
Beelzebub called for his syllabub in the hotel in Hell

Where Proserpine first fell,

Blue as the gendarmerie were the waves of the sea,

(Rocking and shocking the bar-maid).

Nobody comes to give him his rum but the
Rim of the sky hippopotamus-glum
Enhances the chances to bless with a benison
Alfred Lord Tennyson crossing the bar laid
With cold vegetation from pale deputations
Of temperance workers (all signed In Memoriam)
Hoping with glory to trip up the Laureate's feet,

(Moving in classical metres) . . .

Like Balaclava, the lava came down from the
Roof, and the sea's blue wooden gendarmerie
Took them in charge while Beelzebub roared for his
rum.
. . . None of them come!

THE BAT

EDITH
SITWELL

Castellated, tall
From battlements fall
Shades on heroic
Lonely grass,
Where the moonlight's echoes die and pass.
Near the rustic boorish,
Fustian Moorish,
Castle wall of the ultimate Shade,
With his cloak castellated as that wall, afraid,
The mountebank doctor,
The old stage quack,
Where decoy duck dust
Began to clack,
Watched Heliogabalusene the Bat
In his furred cloak hang head down from the flat
Wall, cling to what is convenient,
Lenient.
'If you hang upside down with squeaking shrill,
You will see dust, lust, and the will to kill,
And life is a matter of which way falls
Your tufted turreted Shade near these walls.
For muttering guttering shadow will plan
If you're ruined wall, or pygmy man,'
Said Heliogabalusene, 'or a pig,
Or the empty Cæsar in tall periwig.'
And the mountebank doctor,
The old stage quack,
Spread out a black membraned wing of his cloak
And his shuffling footsteps seem to choke,
Near the Castle wall of the ultimate Shade
Where decoy duck dust
Quacks, clacks, afraid.

THE FARNESE HERCULES

Heroes out of music born
March their glittering shades down myrtle alleys in the
    poet's wood
Breaking the rhymed lights of reason:
For these three lines of preface
The black cape of magic hides my head and hands
Till I fix the staring camera eye:
'Keep that position, gentlemen! keep it and look
    pleasant!'
The chattering agora, sudden camp of stalls,
Reaches to the statue's feet, to the platform for these
    stylites,
Who stand all day and night in rain's blue cage,   10
Fed with this water and the yellow bread of sun.

'It will make a very pretty water-colour.
Look how still he keeps. Tie your sandal to his ankle.'
He was one among a whole white wood of statues
In the market-place along a road of triumph,
Then moved with pulleys at the trumpet's sound
To the Baths of Caracalla where the rhymed lights of
    poetry
Bore the new Prometheus from the womb of that dead
    music.
Hercules lay broken in the heaped, dried dust;
His legs took twenty long years to find   20
So bitter had his fall been. To the roll of thunder
Fell he, or the red Goth's hand?

Now his dwelling is a dark museum,
A dingy hotel dining-room with no food ever served,
We'll forget that dreary future for his laboured past;
We will take him from the Thermae to his native land,
To the poplars and the caverns, to the hills of wild
    thyme,
Their limestone worn by rain's slow tide
In spires and guttering pinnacles;
No foot climbs to those towers but the bearded goat 30
Cropping the cold herb among the cactus swords,
While winds of prophecy in hollow caves foment
To break from the shepherd's lips, or speak by signs.

The agora, that platform for the quack and the actor,
For anyone swollen with the wind of talk,
Grew to a parliament of all the muses,
Till poetry and music, spawn of words, were born
And gods walked in the harvest, or among the grapes,
To choose a mirror of themselves in men;
They tired of immortal love and stole into the harvest
Hidden in wind's raiment, or at a tower of stone   41
Fell in a gold shower like sun with rain;
Such were the loves of gods who schemed in green
    barley
To snare the bowed reapers, or grape-gatherers on
    their ladders.

This talking, ceaseless talking, like a rookery in the
    elm's green roofs,
Cawed and chattered whilst they built with twigs,
Though here in the agora the twigs were beams of
    marble
And they worked like the rooks do by tradition and
    proportion;
Their temples were a shepherd's hut magnified

With ninepin pillars and a tilted roof   50
Walling in this open way a dark inner mystery.
Since the gods made a mirror of themselves in men,
Sculpture, a shepherd's craft—they carve in their
          waste-hours—
Copied like a camera this echoed immortality
And matched the mortal limbs of man against the
          deathless gods.

Then, the forests of white statues grew
And the gods and men among them only differed in
          their emblems;
The athlete oiled and slippery for wrestling
Stands by a god who treads the windy hills,
You could see this naked athlete in the stadium   60
And hear that god speaking in the groves of philosophy,
His limbs gleaming white from sharp edges of the
          myrtles
In the fainting sunset when the lengthened shades are
          lifted;
Then were those arsenals of legend stored,
The hills of thyme were the stepping-stones to heaven
And the wind spake in oracles from sacred woods.

The normal, the simple life was in the young, fresh air
With the shepherds sitting by their sticks of fire
Or the fisherman living by his nets of fortune
Throwing for fast silver in that tideless sea.   70
It was the Golden Age before the Age of Gold began;
How snow-soft were those legends falling every year
In a winter of white blossoms through the speaking
          trees,
For they formed, like the snow does, to the shapes they
          loved,
To a sliding gentle poetry that is made of nothing,

Though it lives by the body of its melted beauty,
In a sharp, deep river, or at a fountain in the rock.

The tumbrils slowly creaking under pyramids of grapes
That ran down their life-blood on these boards and on
    the oxen
Took home the husbandmen,   80
Maddened by these fumes and by the pulsing sun;
This shadow-life of drunkenness, this mocking of the
    fire of health,
Gave birth with its mirror to a world of ghosts,
The theatre and its actors began at that stained trestle
And masks to keep the mirror truth and hide the living
    difference
Were born in that blue autumn. The mock children
Of fine shepherds and their bearded goats were shown;
And the goat-god in dark rocks once seen.

Where the tumbril waited in the pine-tree shade
They made a trodden dancing-floor,   90
This grew into a half-moon of rough-hewn stone,
To the theatre of mock death and laughter;
There did these ghosts stalk on stilt-like pattens
And thunder the heroic verse through mouths of brass.
In the dun twilight other shadows creep,
While this first giant art is born out of rolling high
    speeches;
Other shadows creep between the syllables
In chequers so that light or shade can hide them,
And Harlequin's wand becomes a thyrsus in the grape-
    harvest.

Thus was the camera eye tricked and cheated,   100
For these ghosts with their masks and stilts were out-
    side life.

Was ever death so cold as this, or love so fiery?
Those armoured gods, those women calm as oxen,
In the cold heroic mazes, in sacred families of tragedy,
Move to their destiny. The beardless ephebus
Comes through the flower-thickets, stands naked in full
    light of day,
For he was the vehicle of their strange loves;
So to those legends we have giant stilted shades,
Ox-eyed women, and young naked limbs
That will tear on a rose-bush, or stain with the grape.

He was born, our Hercules, in the yard of a stone-
    mason,   III
Dragged in his matrix by a team of oxen
And tilted with a lever to that ground thick with
    statues,
There he stands rough and clumsy like a boy on his first
    school day
Waiting for the chisel and the cold eye to study him.
Tie your sandal to his ankle! Tease him like a bear!
Though who can the gipsy be who leads him, ring in
    nose,
By green hedges, his rough bed at night,
To the crowded, noisy agora,
To that theatre where the gipsy's horn   120
Sounds among the shadows that the statues throw?

Twelve labours, twelve slow tours on foot,
Has he who made the beetle walk laid out before him,
Though the labours of Hercules are tasks he can't
    avoid,
He is carried there by instinct like dogs to a dog-fight.
Instinct, little voice, scarce seen, scarce felt,
Like the Indian on his elephant who guides it with a
    whisper

And can ride in a castle on that patient wave-back
Through green waters of the Indian bright boughs;
So, turned gipsy to our Hercules
We will walk in the dew-deep orchard
Tasting apples of Hesperides.

Tie your sandal to his ankle! He will be your winged
     Mercury
To run before you. Won't he move? Won't he stir?
He is dank, cold, and dewy like mushrooms of the
     night
Spawned in summer showers from goatskins of the
     rain;
He leans on his truncheon like a great policeman.
Glycon was his sculptor, and Lysippus before him
Had planned this demi-god leaning weary on his club;
Lysippus of Sicyon with his fifteen hundred shapes of
     stone   140
Who wrought his white nightmares like the sculptors
     of Carrara
From the salt-white quarries;—
While Glycon had the Romans for his Yankee patrons.

At least there was never such a gladiator:—
Or there'd be no audience in the Roman theatre;
He'd eat them up like paper!
No hero on wars of love in the wood's green tent
Ever heard the nightingales, bright stars to such an
     armour;
Had he lulled, my Hercules, below these lights
That sang in wan air   150
Before the moon in green tree-windows,
The glitter, while he slept, that should have touched
     his steel

Would lie on no armour but his heaped rings of
muscle,
Rocks deep-hidden in a sea of smooth skin.

He should be the sentinel on cyclopaean walls
Guarding a megalithic rock-hewn town
And moved to ram's-horn trumpet, blown
At the tomb-mouth lintel of that city-gate;
He is watching the flocks of sheep, dropped petals from
the clouds
That move with shadow-stilts along the hill's green
sides,   160
Or he guards the hayricks, honeystacks of grass,
That are pitched like a shepherd's hut with high,
sloped roof
And yet are combs of honey that are cut for the cattle,
For they store all the yellow light that fed the grass
And hold sun and rain within their golden straws.

These villages of giant stone spread like a fashion
From mouth to mouth of shepherds
As by beacons on high, lonely hills;
Temples like giant hearthstones are built on the bare
plains
And they save up their captives for the sacrifice of fire
When they burn a wicker tower of them above the
stones.   171
That was a Golden Age for Hercules,
On wrestling ground, or at rough bed of leaves,
In fleecy nights of winter
Wrapped in woven wool as white as they,
When breath turns to smoke.

See him throw stones to keep the rooks off the barley!
They start quite low and rise on a parabola,

They blossom at their zenith, shut their wings into a
    meteor,
And fall like an anchor out of the clouds among the
    rooks. 180
See him run to turn the drove of horses!
He can blow in a corner of the barley
And bend that sunny hair against the wind,
So the reaper with his sickle cuts two sheaves for one;
Those horses that he turned and headed
Gallop in front of Hercules like a drum shower of the
    rain
Falling on loud leaves and the thatched hair of houses.

Hercules as husbandman is in the grapes,
He pulls the blue bunches from their roof of leaves
To fill the wicker baskets that the women hold 190
And they spill them into a pyramid in a space between
    the vines:
It towers like a summer wave full of the sun,
Could this be still and frozen for a word to break;
Then into that deep sea of sun and summer rain
He wades and treads until its fire is loosed;
The rocks and hollow hills echo with his laughter,
Rocks that are the cold bed for goat-foot gods,
And caves, old mirrors for their sighs and loves.

The kneeling, fainting cherry trees,
So deep their green sails and their mouths of fire 200
That they burn like a galleon to the water-line,
Kiss with red lips his hands
That feel among the apple-trees
To their branches heavy with those sweets of rain.
Who knows what voices rang among the boughs
When limbs, so light they were like the wind between
    the leaves,

Climbed from cool water,
And the orchard, one green tree of birds,
Sang from every window in its sunny leaves?

Cunning or big muscle were the ways to power,   21(
To the Emperor lifted on a shield in the camp,
Till the Hebrew prophet and the fishermen;—
Then the men of destiny like old idols were thrown
     down
And the trumpets of triumph became horns at the
     tournament;
The walls of the castle like white cliffs of chalk
Stood like bulwarks to the green sea of time:
Long Gothic faces of the fair-haired warriors
Showed from beetle armour for those glitters down the
     myrtle glade:
Those ancient heroes to long trees of birth
Surrendered, and the herald's horns.   22 (

Now there'd be no use for him, no work for Hercules,
Unless he turned policeman
And joined the Irish bullies on loud Broadway;
He could part the streams of traffic with a white-gloved
     hand
And snare the gunmen in their stolen motor;
Glycon and Lysippus would be sad to see him
With his fugal muscles in neat armour of blue cloth.
Away with him! Roll him to the drab museum,
To the stone companionship of other shades:
Let there be a banquet of the gods   23 (
On tired air through tangled, cobweb windows!

He lives again in thin shade of the olive-trees
At a cold fountain in the rocks
Watering his oxen;

From the orchard walled with river stones
Apples of sweet rain hang forth
While kneeling, fainting cherry trees bleed fire on to
    the grass:
Let those green wings of the wind, sharp leaves,
Give him music for his feasting,
While fine nymphs of the river from their sighing
    brakes 240
Climb into the orchard, where great Hercules
Sleeps by sweet rain boughs and by cherry mouths of
    fire.

RICHARD EBERHART

THE GROUNDHOG

In June, amid the golden fields,
I saw a groundhog lying dead.
Dead lay he; my senses shook,
And mind outshot our naked frailty.
There lowly in the vigorous summer
His form began its senseless change,
And made my senses waver dim
Seeing nature ferocious in him.
Inspecting close his maggot's might
And seething cauldron of his being,
Half with loathing, half with a strange love,
I poked him with an angry stick.
The fever arose, became a frame
And Vigour circumscribed the skies,
Immense energy in the sun,
And through my flame a sunless trembling.
My stick had done nor good nor harm.
Then stood I silent in the day
Watching the object, as before;
And kept my reverence for knowledge
Trying for control, to be still,
To quell the passion of the blood;
Until I had bent down on my knees
Praying for joy in the sight of decay.
And so I left; and I returned
In Autumn strict of eye, to see
The sap gone out of the groundhog,
But the bony sodden hulk remained.
But the year had lost its meaning,

And in intellectual chains
I lost both love and loathing,
Mured up in the wall of wisdom.
Another summer took the fields again
Massive and burning, full of life,
But when I chanced upon the spot
There was only a little hair left,
And bones bleaching in the sunlight
Beautiful as architecture;
I watched them like a geometer,
And cut a walking stick from a birch.
It has been three years, now.
There is no sign of the groundhog.
I stood there in the whirling summer,
My hand capped a withered heart,
And thought of China and of Greece,
Of Alexander in his tent;
Of Montaigne in his tower,
Of Saint Theresa in her wild lament.

PETER QUENNELL

HERO ENTOMBED (I)

My lamp, full charged with its sweet oil, still burns,
Has burned a whole year and it shows no check.
My cerements there
Lie where I rolled them off,
The death odours within them,
Harshly composed, coiled up in marble fold.

This tent of white translucent stone, my tomb,
Lets through its panel such a ray of light,
Blind and refracted,
As a calm sea might do
Through its tough warping lens
From the ascendant moon at its highest step.

Some have complained the gentleness of the sea,
Stagnantly streaming, in quick ebb withdrawing
Along the tideless South,
Thus sound to me,
And like its noonday hiss
Wheels, voices, music, thunder, the trumpet at dawn

You must not think my entertainment slight
In the close prison where I walk all day.
'And yet, entombed,
Do not your thoughts oppressed
Pluck off the bandage from your sores,
From arrow wound and from ulcered armour-gall?'

My wounds are dried already to pale weals,
I did not fall in battle as you think,

On Epipolae
Dashed from the rock head down,
Or in the quarries stifle,
But stoned by words and pierced with beams of eyes.

PETER
QUEN-
NELL

So, patient, not regretful, self consoling
I walk, touching the tomb wall with my fingers,
In silent entertainment.
On the smooth floor
The stirred dust ankle deep
Steams up languid, to clog the struggling lamp flame.

Syracuse

THE FLIGHT INTO EGYPT

Within Heaven's circle I had not guessed at this,
I had not guessed at pleasure such as this,
So sharp a pleasure,
That, like a lamp burning in foggy night,
Makes its own orb and sphere of flowing gold
And tents itself in light.

Going before you, now how many days,
Thoughts, all turned back like birds against the wind,
Wheeled sullenly towards my Father's house,
Considered his blind presence and the gathered,
        bustling pæan,
The affluence of his sweetness, his grace and unageing
        might.

My flesh glowed then in the shadow of a loose cloak
And my brightness troubled the ground with every
        pulse of the blood,
My wings lax on the air, my eyes open and grave,
With the vacant pride of hardly less than a god.

251

PETER We passed thickets that quaked with hidden deer,
QUEN- And wide shallows dividing before my feet,
NELL Empty plains threaded, and between stiff aloes
      I took the ass's bridle to climb into mountain path-
          ways.

When cold bit you, through your peasant's mantle,
And my Father filled the air with meaningless stars,
I brought dung and dead white grass for fuel,
Blowing a fire with the breath of the holy word.

Your drudge, Joseph, slept; you would sit unmoving,
In marble quiet, or by the unbroken voice of a river,
Would sometimes bare your maiden breast to his
      mouth,
The suckling, to the conscious God balanced upon your
      knees.

Apart I considered the melodious names of my
      brothers,
As again in my Father's house, and the even spheres
Slowly, nightlong recalled the splendour of numbers;
I heard again the voluptuous measure of praise.

Sometimes pacing beneath clarity immeasurable
I saw my mind lie open and desert,
The wavering streams frozen up and each coppice
      quieted,
A whole valley in starlight with leaves and waters.

Coming at last to these farthest Syrian hills,
Attis or Adon, some ambushed lust looked out;
My skin grows pale and smooth, shrunken as silk,
Without the rough effulgence of a God.

And here no voice has spoken;
There is no shrine of any godhead here;

No grove or hallowed fires,
And godhead seems asleep.

PETER
QUEN-
NELL

Only the vine has woven
Strange houses and blind rooms and palaces,
Into each hollow and crevice continually
Dropped yearlong irrecoverable flowers.

The sprawling vine has built us a close room;
Obedient Hymen fills the air with mist;
And to make dumb our theft
The white and moving sand that will not bear a print.

PROCNE

So she became a bird and bird-like danced
On a long sloe-bough, treading the silver blossom
With a bird's lovely feet,
And shaken blossoms fell into the hands
Of sunlight, and he held them for a moment
And let them drop.
And in the autumn Procne came again
And leapt upon the crooked sloe-bough singing
And the dark berries winked like earth-dimmed beads,
As the branch swung beneath her dancing feet.

WILLIAM EMPSON

THE SCALES

The proper scale would pat you on the head
But Alice showed her pup Ulysses' bough
Well from behind a thistle, wise with dread;

And though your gulf-sprung mountains I allow
(Snow-puppy curves, rose-solemn dado band)
Charming for nurse, I am not nurse just now.

Why pat or stride them, when the train will land
Me high, through climbing tunnels, at your side,
And careful fingers meet through castle sand.

Claim slyly rather that the tunnels hide
Solomon's gems, white vistas, preserved kings,
By jackal sandhole to your aim flung wide.

Say (she suspects) to sea Nile only brings
Delta and indecision, who instead
Far back up country does enormous things.

INVITATION TO JUNO

WILLIAM
EMPSON

Lucretius could not credit centaurs;
Such bicycle he deemed asynchronous.
'Man superannuates the horse;
Horse pulses will not gear with ours.'

Johnson could see no bicycle would go;
'You bear yourself, and the machine as well.'
Gennets for germans sprang not from Othello,
And Ixion rides upon a single wheel.

Courage. Weren't strips of heart culture seen
Of late mating two periodicities?
Could not Professor Charles Darwin
Graft annual upon perennial trees?

CAMPING OUT

And now she cleans her teeth into the lake:
Gives it (God's grace) for her own bounty's sake
What morning's pale and the crisp mist debars:
Its glass of the divine (that Will could break)
Restores, beyond Nature: or lets Heaven take
(Itself being dimmed) her pattern, who half awake
Milks between rocks a straddled sky of stars.

Soap tension the star pattern magnifies.
Smoothly Madonna through-assumes the skies
Whose vaults are opened to achieve the Lord.
No, it is we soaring explore galaxies,
Our bullet boat light's speed by thousands flies.
Who moves so among stars their frame unties;
See where they blur, and die, and are outsoared.

LEGAL FICTION

Law makes long spokes of the short stakes of men.
Your well fenced out real estate of mind
No high flat of the nomad citizen
Looks over, or train leaves behind.

Your rights extend under and above your claim
Without bound; you own land in Heaven and Hell;
Your part of earth's surface and mass the same,
Of all cosmos' volume, and all stars as well.

Your rights reach down where all owners meet, in
    Hell's
Pointed exclusive conclave, at earth's centre
(Your spun farm's root still on that axis dwells);
And up, through galaxies, a growing sector.

You are nomad yet; the lighthouse beam you own
Flashes, like Lucifer, through the firmament.
Earth's axis varies; your dark central cone
Wavers, a candle's shadow, at the end.

THIS LAST PAIN

This last pain for the damned the Fathers found:
'They knew the bliss with which they were not
    crowned.'
    Such, but on earth, let me foretell,
    Is all, of heaven or of hell.

Man, as the prying housemaid of the soul,
May know her happiness by eye to hole:
    He's safe; the key is lost; he knows
    Door will not open, nor hole close.

'What is conceivable can happen too,'
Said Wittgenstein, who had not dreamt of you;
  But wisely; if we worked it long
  We should forget where it was wrong:

Those thorns are crowns which, woven into knots,
Crackle under and soon boil fools' pots;
  And no man's watching, wise and long,
  Would ever stare them into song.

Thorns burn to a consistent ash, like man;
A splendid cleanser for the frying-pan:
  And those who leap from pan to fire
  Should this brave opposite admire.

All those large dreams by which men long live well
Are magic-lanterned on the smoke of hell;
  This then is real, I have implied,
  A painted, small, transparent slide.

These the inventive can hand-paint at leisure,
Or most emporia would stock our measure;
  And feasting in their dappled shade
  We should forget how they were made.

Feign then what's by a decent tact believed
And act that state is only so conceived,
  And build an edifice of form
  For house where phantoms may keep warm.

Imagine, then, by miracle, with me,
(Ambiguous gifts, as what gods give must be)
  What could not possibly be there,
  And learn a style from a despair.

HOMAGE TO THE BRITISH MUSEUM

There is a supreme God in the ethnological section;
A hollow toad shape, faced with a blank shield.
He needs his belly to include the Pantheon,
Which is inserted through a hole behind.
At the navel, at the points formally stressed, at the
    organs of sense,
Lice glue themselves, dolls, local deities,
His smooth wood creeps with all the creeds of the
    world.

Attending there let us absorb the cultures of nations
And dissolve into our judgement all their codes.
Then, being clogged with a natural hesitation
(People are continually asking one the way out),
Let us stand here and admit that we have no road.
Being everything, let us admit that is to be something,
Or give ourselves the benefit of the doubt;
Let us offer our pinch of dust all to this God,
And grant his reign over the entire building.

NOTE ON LOCAL FLORA

There is a tree native in Turkestan,
Or further east towards the Tree of Heaven,
Whose hard cold cones, not being wards to time,
Will leave their mother only for good cause;
Will ripen only in a forest fire;
Wait, to be fathered as was Bacchus once,
Through men's long lives, that image of time's end.
I knew the Phœnix was a vegetable.
So Semele desired her deity
As this in Kew thirsts for the Red Dawn.

C. DAY LEWIS

'IT IS BECOMING NOW TO DECLARE MY ALLEGIANCE'

It is becoming now to declare my allegiance,
To dig some reservoir for my springtime's pain,
Bewilderment and pride, before their insurgence
Is all sopped up in this dry regimen.

Laughable dwarfs, you may twirl and tweak my heart,—
Have I not fought with Anakim at the crossways?
Once I was Cicero, though pedant fate
Now bids me learn the grammar of my days.

These, then, have my allegiance; they whose shining
Convicted my false dawn of flagrant night,
Yet ushered up the sun, as poets leaning
Upon a straw surmise the infinite.

You, first, who ground my lust to love upon
Your gritty humorous virginity,
Then yielding to its temper suddenly
Proved what a Danube can be struck from stone:
With you I ran the gauntlet for my prime,
Then living in the moment lived for all time.

Next the hawk-faced man, who could praise an apple
In terms of peach and win the argument. Quick
Was he to trip the shambling rhetoric
Of laws and lions: yet abstract turned the tables
And his mind, almost, with a whiff of air
Clothed first in a woman and after in a nightmare.

She next, sorrow's familiar, who turned
Her darkness to our light; that 'brazen leech'
Alleviating the vain cosmic itch
With fact coated in formulæ lest it burned
Our tongue. She shall have portion in my praise,
And live in me, not memory, for always.

Last the tow-haired poet, never done
With cutting and planing some new gnomic prop
To jack his all too stable universe up:—
Conduct's Old Dobbin, thought's chameleon.
Single mind copes with split intelligence,
Breeding a piebald strain of truth and nonsense.

These have I loved and chosen, once being sure
Some spacious vision waved upon their eyes
That troubles not the common register;
And love them still, knowing it otherwise.

Knowing they held no mastership in wisdom
Or wit save by certificate of my love,
I have found out a better way to praise them—
Nestor shall die and let Patroclus live.

So I declare it. These are they who built
My house and never a stone of it laid agley.
So cheat I memory that works in gilt
And stucco to restore a fallen day.

'SUPPOSE THAT WE'

Suppose that we, to-morrow or the next day,
Came to an end—in storm the shafting broken,
Or a mistaken signal, the flange lifting—
Would that be premature, a text for sorrow?

Say what endurance gives or death denies us.
Love's proved in its creation, not eternity:
Like leaf or linnet the true heart's affection
Is born, dies later, asks no reassurance.

C. Day
Lewis

Over dark wood rises one dawn felicitous,
Bright through awakened shadows fall her crystal
Cadenzas, and once for all the wood is quickened.
So our joys visit us, and it suffices.

Nor fear we now to live who in the valley
Of the shadow of life have found a causeway;
For love restores the nerve and love is under
Our feet resilient. Shall we be weary?

Some say we walk out of Time altogether
This way into a region where the primrose
Shows an immortal dew, sun at meridian
Stands up for ever and in scent the lime tree.

This is a land which later we may tell of.
Here-now we know, what death cannot diminish
Needs no replenishing; yet certain are, though
Dying were well enough, to live is better.

Passion has grown full man by his first birthday.
Running across the bean-fields in a south wind,
Fording the river mouth to feel the tide-race—
Child's play that was, though proof of our possessions.

Now our research is done, measured the shadow,
The plains mapped out, the hills a natural bound'ry.
Such and such is our country. There remains to
Plough up the meadowland, reclaim the marshes.

'AS ONE WHO WANDERS INTO OLD WORKINGS'

As one who wanders into old workings
Dazed by the noonday, desiring coolness,
Has found retreat barred by fall of rockface;
Gropes through galleries where granite bruises
Taut palm and panic patters close at heel;
Must move forward as tide to the moon's nod,
As mouth to breast in blindness is beckoned.
Nightmare nags at his elbow and narrows
Horizon to pinpoint, hope to hand's breadth.
Slow drip the seconds, time is stalactite,
For nothing intrudes here to tell the time,
Sun marches not, nor moon with muffled step.
He wants an opening,—only to break out,
To see the dark glass cut by day's diamond,
To relax again in the lap of light.

But we seek a new world through old workings,
Whose hope lies like seed in the loins of earth,
Whose dawn draws gold from the roots of darkness.
Not shy of light nor shrinking from shadow
Like Jesuits in jungle we journey
Deliberately bearing to brutish tribes
Christ's assurance, arts of agriculture.
As a train that travels underground track
Feels current flashed from far-off dynamos,
Our wheels whirling with impetus elsewhere
Generated we run, are ruled by rails.
Train shall spring from tunnel to terminus,
Out on to plain shall the pioneer plunge,
Earth reveal what veins fed, what hill covered.
Lovely the leap, explosion into light.

'DO NOT EXPECT AGAIN A PHŒNIX HOUR'

C. Day Lewis

Do not expect again a phœnix hour,
The triple-towered sky, the dove complaining,
Sudden the rain of gold and heart's first ease
Tranced under trees by the eldritch light of sundown.

By a blazed trail our joy will be returning:
One burning hour throws light a thousand ways,
And hot blood stays into familiar gestures.
The best years wait, the body's plenitude.

Consider then, my lover, this is the end
Of the lark's ascending, the hawk's unearthly hover:
Spring season is over soon and first heatwave;
Grave-browed with cloud ponders the huge horizon.

Draw up the dew. Swell with pacific violence.
Take shape in silence. Grow as the clouds grew.
Beautiful brood the cornlands, and you are heavy;
Leafy the boughs—they also hide big fruit.

'COME OUT IN THE SUN'

Come out in the sun, for a man is born to-day!
Early this morning whistle in the cutting told
Train was arriving, hours overdue, delayed
By snow-drifts, engine-trouble, Act of God, who cares
        now?—
For here alights the distinguished passenger.
Take a whole holiday in honour of this!

Kipfer's back from heaven, Bendien to Holland,
Larwood and Voce in the Notts eleven.

C. Day
Lewis
Returning also the father the mother
Chastened and cheered by underworld excursion,
Alive returning from the black country,
Take a whole holiday in honour of this.

Now shall the airman vertically banking
Out of the blue write a new sky-sign;
The nine tramp steamers rusting in the estuary
Get up full pressure for a trade revival;
The crusty landlord renew the lease, and everyone
Take a whole holiday in honour of this.

To-day let director forget the deficit,
Schoolmaster his handicap, hostess her false face:
Let phantasist take charge of flesh-and-blood situation,
Petty-officer be rapt in the Seventh Symphony.
For here a champion is born and commands you
Take a whole holiday in honour of this.

Wherever radiance from ashes arises—
Willowherb glowing on abandoned slagheaps,
Dawn budding scarlet in a bed of darkness,
Life from exhausted womb outstriving—
There shall the spirit be lightened and gratefully
Take a whole holiday in honour of this.

'YOU THAT LOVE ENGLAND'

You that love England, who have an ear for her music,
The slow movement of clouds in benediction,
Clear arias of light thrilling over her uplands,
Over the chords of summer sustained peacefully;
Ceaseless the leaves' counterpoint in a west wind
    lively,

Blossom and river rippling loveliest allegro,   C. DAY
And the storms of wood strings brass at year's finale: LEWIS
Listen. Can you not hear the entrance of a new theme?

You who go out alone, on tandem or on pillion,
Down arterial roads riding in April,
Or sad beside lakes where hill-slopes are reflected
Making fires of leaves, your high hopes fallen:
Cyclists and hikers in company, day excursionists,
Refugees from cursed towns and devastated areas;
Know you seek a new world, a saviour to establish
Long-lost kinship and restore the blood's fulfilment.

You who like peace, good sticks, happy in a small way
Watching birds or playing cricket with schoolboys,
Who pay for drinks all round, whom disaster chose
     not;
Yet passing derelict mills and barns roof-rent
Where despair has burnt itself out—hearts at a stand-
     still,
Who suffer loss, aware of lowered vitality;
We can tell you a secret, offer a tonic; only
Submit to the visiting angel, the strange new healer.

You above all who have come to the far end, victims
Of a run-down machine, who can bear it no longer;
Whether in easy chairs chafing at impotence
Or against hunger, bullies and spies preserving
The nerve for action, the spark of indignation—
Need fight in the dark no more, you know your
     enemies.
You shall be leaders when zero hour is signalled,
Wielders of power and welders of a new world.

THE CONFLICT

I sang as one
Who on a tilting deck sings
To keep their courage up, though the wave hangs
That shall cut off their sun.

As storm-cocks sing,
Flinging their natural answer in the wind's teeth,
And care not if it is waste of breath
Or birth-carol of spring.

As ocean-flyer clings
To height, to the last drop of spirit driving on
While yet ahead is land to be won
And work for wings.

Singing I was at peace,
Above the clouds, outside the ring:
For sorrow finds a swift release in song
And pride its poise.

Yet living here,
As one between two massing powers I live
Whom neutrality cannot save
Nor occupation cheer.

None such shall be left alive:
The innocent wing is soon shot down,
And private stars fade in the blood-red dawn
Where two worlds strive.

The red advance of life
Contracts pride, calls out the common blood,
Beats song into a single blade,
Makes a depth-charge of grief.

Move then with new desires,
For where we used to build and love
Is no man's land, and only ghosts can live
Between two fires.

A TIME TO DANCE

For those who had the power
   of the forest fires that burn
Leaving their source in ashes
   to flush the sky with fire:
Those whom a famous urn
   could not contain, whose passion
Brimmed over the deep grave
   and dazzled epitaphs:
For all that have won us wings
   to clear the tops of grief,
My friend who within me laughs
   bids you dance and sing.

Some set out to explore
   earth's limit, and little they recked if
Never their feet came near it
   outgrowing the need for glory:
Some aimed at a small objective
   but the fierce updraught of their spirit
Forced them to the stars.
   Are honoured in public who built
The dam that tamed a river;
   or holding the salient for hours
Against odds, cut off and killed,
   are remembered by one survivor.

All these. But most for those
   whom accident made great,

As a radiant chance encounter
    of cloud and sunlight grows
Immortal on the heart:
    whose gift was the sudden bounty
Of a passing moment, enriches
    the fulfilled eye for ever.
Their spirits float serene
    above time's roughest reaches,
But their seed is in us and over
    our lives they are evergreen.

From THE FLIGHT

(*'Sing we the two Lieutenants, Parer and M'Intosh'*)

And now the earth they had spurned rose up against
    them in anger,
Tier upon tier it towered, the terrible Apennines:
No sanctuary there for wings, not flares nor landing-
    lines,
No hope of floor and hangar.
Yet those ice-tipped spears that disputed the passage set
    spurs
To their two hundred and forty horse power; grimly
    they gained
Altitude, though the hand of heaven was heavy upon
    them,
The downdraught from the mountains: though
    desperate eddies spun them
Like a coin, yet unkindly tossed their luck came upper-
    most
And mastery remained.

Air was all ambushes round them, was avalanche earth-
Quicksand, a funnel deep as doom, till climbing steep
They crawled like a fly up the face of perpendicular
    night
And levelled, finding a break
At fourteen thousand feet. Here earth is shorn from
    sight:
Deadweight a darkness hangs on their eyelids, and they
    bruise
Their eyes against a void: vindictive the cold airs close
Down like a trap of steel and numb them from head to
    heel;
Yet they kept an even keel,
For their spirit reached forward and took the controls
    while their fingers froze.

They had not heard the last of death. When the
    mountains were passed,
He raised another crest, the long crescendo of pain
Kindled to climax, the plane
Took fire. Alone in the sky with the breath of their
    enemy
Hot in their face they fought: from three thousand feet
    they tilted
Over, side-slipped away—a trick for an ace, a race
And running duel with death: flame streamed out
    behind,
A crimson scarf of, as life-blood out of a wound, but
    the wind
Of their downfall staunched it; death wilted,
Lagged and died out in smoke—he could not stay their
    pace.

A lull for a while. The powers of hell rallied their
legions.
   On Parer now fell the stress of the flight; for the plane
      had been bumped,
   Buffeted, thrashed by the air almost beyond repair:
   But he tinkered and coaxed, and they limped
   Over the Adriatic on into warmer regions.
   Erratic their course to Athens, to Crete: coolly they
      rode her
   Like a tired horse at the water-jumps, they jockeyed
      her over seas,
   Till they came at last to a land whose dynasties of sand
   Had seen Alexander, Napoleon, many a straddling
      invader,
   But never none like these.

   England to Cairo, a joy-ride, a forty-hour journey at
      most,
   Had cost them forty-four days. What centuried strata
      of life
   Fuelled the fire that haled them to heaven, the power
      that held them
   Aloft? For their plane was a laugh,
   A patch, brittle as matchstick, a bubble, a lift for a
      ghost:
   Bolts always working loose of propeller, cylinder,
      bearer;
   Instruments faulty; filter, magneto, each strut
      unsound.
   Yet after four days, though we swore she never could
      leave the ground,
   We saw her in headstrong haste diminish towards the
      east—
   That makeshift, mad sky-farer.

Aimed they now for Baghdad, unwritten in air's annals C. DAY
A voyage. But theirs the fate all flights of logic to   LEWIS
    refute,
Who obeyed no average law, who buoyed the viewless
    channels
Of sky with a courage steadfast, luminous. Safe they
    crossed
Sinai's desert, and daring
The Nejd, the unneighbourly waste of Arabia, yet
    higher soaring
(Final a fall there for birds of passage, limed and lost
In shifty the sand's embrace) all day they strove to
    climb
Through stormy rain: but they felt her shorten her
    stride and falter,
And they fell at evening time.

Slept that night beside their machine, and the next
    morning
Raider Arabs appeared reckoning this stranded bird
A gift: like cobras they struck, and their gliding
    shadows athwart
The sand were all their warning.
But the aeronauts, knowing iron the coinage here, had
    brought
Mills bombs and revolvers, and M'Intosh held them off
While Parer fought for life—
A spark, the mechanic's right answer, and finally
    wrought
A miracle, for the dumb engine spoke and they rose
Convulsively out of the clutch of the desert, the clench
    of their foes.

. . . .

271

C. Day
Lewis
And they picked her up out of it somehow and put her
at the air, a
Sorry hack for such steeplechasing, to leap the sky.
'We'll fly this bloody crate till it falls to bits at our
feet,'
Said the mechanic Parer.
And at Moulmein soon they crashed; and the plane by
their spirit's high
Tension long pinned, girded and guarded from dis-
solution,
Fell to bits at their feet. Wrecked was the under-
carriage,
Radiator cracked, in pieces, compasses crocked;
Fallen all to confusion.
Their winged hope was a heap of scrap, but un-
splintered their courage.

Six weeks they worked in sun-glare and jungle damps,
assembling
Fragments to make airworthy what was worth not its
weight in air.
As a surgeon, grafter of skin, as a setter of bones
tumbling
Apart, they had power to repair
This good for naught but the grave: they livened her
engine and gave
Fuselage faith to rise rejuvenated from ruin.
Went with them stowaways, not knowing what hazard
they flew in—
Bear-cubs, a baby alligator, lizards and snakes galore;
Mascots maybe, for the plane though twice she was
floored again
Always came up for more.

Till they came to the pitiless mountains of Timor. Yet
  these, untamed,
Not timorous, against the gradient and Niagara of air
  they climbed
Scarce-skimming the summits; and over the shark-
  toothed Timor sea
Lost their bearings, but shirked not the odds, the
  deaths that lurked
A million to one on their trail:
They reached out to the horizon and plucked their
  destiny.
On for eight hours they flew blindfold against the
  unknown,
And the oil began to fail
And their flying spirit waned—one pint of petrol
  remained
When the land stood up to meet them and they came
  into their own.

Southward still to Melbourne, the bourn of their
  flight, they pressed
Till at last near Culcairn, like a last fretted leaf
Falling from brave autumn into earth's breast,
D.H. nine, their friend that had seen them to the end,
Gave up her airy life.
The Southern Cross was splendid above the spot where
  she fell,
The end of her rainbow curve over our weeping day:
And the flyers, glad to be home, unharmed by that
  dizzy fall,
Dazed as the dead awoken from death, stepped out of
  the broken
Body and went away.

W. H. AUDEN

PROLOGUE

O love, the interest itself in thoughtless Heaven
Make simpler daily the beating of man's heart; within
There in the ring where name and image meet

Inspire them with such a longing as will make his
     thought
Alive like patterns a murmuration of starlings
Rising in joy over wolds unwittingly weave;

Here too on our little reef display your power,
This fortress perched on the edge of the Atlantic scarp
The mole between all Europe and the exile-crowded
     sea;

And make us as Newton was who in his garden watch-
     ing
The apple falling towards England became aware
Between himself and her of an eternal tie.

For now that dream which so long has contented our
     will,
I mean, of uniting the dead into a splendid empire,
Under whose fertilising flood the Lancashire moss

Sprouted up chimneys and Glamorgan hid a life
Grim as a tidal rock-pool's in its glove-shaped valleys,
Is already retreating into her maternal shadow;

Leaving the furnaces gasping in the impossible air
The flotsam at which Dumbarton gapes and hungers,
While upon wind-loved Rowley no hammer shakes

The cluster of mounds like a midget golf course,
    graves
Of some who created these intelligible dangerous
    marvels;
Affectionate people, but crude their sense of glory.

Far-sighted as falcons, they looked down another
    future.
For the seed in their loins were hostile, though afraid
    of their pride,
And tall with a shadow now, inertly wait

In bar, in netted chicken-farm, in lighthouse,
Standing on these impoverished constricting acres,
The ladies and gentlemen apart, too much alone.

Consider the years of the measured world begun,
The barren spiritual marriage of stone and water.
Yet, O, at this very moment of our hopeless sigh

When inland they are thinking their thoughts but are
    watching these islands
As children in Chester look to Moel Fammau to decide
On picnics by the clearness or withdrawal of her tree-
    less crown,

Some dream, say yes, long coiled in the ammonite's
    slumber
Is uncurling, prepared to lay on our talk and kindness
Its military silence, its surgeon's idea of pain.

And called out of tideless peace by a living sun
As when Merlin, tamer of horses, and his lords to
    whom
Stonehenge was still a thought, the Pillars passed

275

And into the undared ocean swung north their prow,
Drives through the night and star-concealing dawn
For the virgin roadsteads of our hearts an unwavering
keel.

'WATCH ANY DAY'

Watch any day his nonchalant pauses, see
His dextrous handling of a wrap as he
Steps after into cars, the beggar's envy.

'There is a free one' many say, but err.
He is not that returning conqueror,
Nor ever the poles' circumnavigator.

But poised between shocking falls on razor-edge
Has taught himself this balancing subterfuge
Of the accosting profile, the erect carriage.

The song, the varied action of the blood
Would drown the warning from the iron wood
Would cancel the inertia of the buried:

Travelling by daylight on from house to house
The longest way to the intrinsic peace,
With love's fidelity and with love's weakness.

'ON SUNDAY WALKS'

On Sunday walks
Past the shut gates of works
The conquerors come
And are handsome.

Sitting all day

W. H.
AUDEN

By the open window
Say what they say
Know what to know
Who brought and taught
Unusual images
And new tunes to old cottages,
With so much done
Without a thought
Of the anonymous lampoon
The cellar counterplot,
Though in the night
Pursued by eaters
They clutch at gaiters
That straddle and deny
Escape that way,
Though in the night
Is waking fright.

Father by son
Lives on and on
Though over date
And motto on the gate
The lichen grows
From year to year,
Still here and there
That Roman nose
Is noticed in the villages
And father's son
Knows what they said
And what they did.

Not meaning to deceive,
Wish to give suck
Enforces make-believe

And what was fear
Of fever and bad-luck
Is now a scare
At certain names
A need for charms
For certain words
At certain fords
And what was livelihood
Is tallness, strongness
Words and longness,
All glory and all story
Solemn and not so good.

'TALLER TO-DAY, WE REMEMBER'

Taller to-day, we remember similar evenings,
Walking together in the windless orchard
Where the brook runs over the gravel, far from the
glacier.

Again in the room with the sofa hiding the grate,
Look down to the river when the rain is over,
See him turn to the window, hearing our last
Of Captain Ferguson.

It is seen how excellent hands have turned to
commonness.
One staring too long, went blind in a tower,
One sold all his manors to fight, broke through, and
faltered.

Nights come bringing the snow, and the dead howl
Under the headlands in their windy dwelling
Because the Adversary put too easy questions
On lonely roads.

But happy now, though no nearer each other,
We see the farms lighted all along the valley;
Down at the mill-shed the hammering stops
And men go home.

Noises at dawn will bring
Freedom for some, but not this peace
No bird can contradict: passing, but is sufficient now
For something fulfilled this hour, loved or endured.

'CONSIDER THIS AND IN OUR TIME'

Consider this and in our time
As the hawk sees it or the helmeted airman:
The clouds rift suddenly—look there
At cigarette-end smouldering on a border
At the first garden party of the year.
Pass on, admire the view of the massif
Through plate-glass windows of the Sport Hotel;
Join there the insufficient units
Dangerous, easy, in furs, in uniform
And constellated at reserved tables
Supplied with feelings by an efficient band
Relayed elsewhere to farmers and their dogs
Sitting in kitchens in the stormy fens.

Long ago, supreme Antagonist,
More powerful than the great northern whale
Ancient and sorry at life's limiting defect,
In Cornwall, Mendip, or the Pennine moor
Your comments on the highborn mining captains,
Found they no answer, made them wish to die
—Lie since in barrows out of harm.
You talk to your admirers every day

W. H.   By silted harbours, derelict works,
AUDEN   In strangled orchards, and the silent comb
        Where dogs have worried or a bird was shot.
        Order the ill that they attack at once:
        Visit the ports and, interrupting
        The leisurely conversation in the bar
        Within a stone's throw of the sunlit water,
        Beckon your chosen out. Summon
        Those handsome and diseased youngsters, those
                women
        Your solitary agents in the country parishes;
        And mobilize the powerful forces latent
        In soils that make the farmer brutal
        In the infected sinus, and the eyes of stoats.
        Then, ready, start your rumour, soft
        But horrifying in its capacity to disgust
        Which, spreading magnified, shall come to be
        A polar peril, a prodigious alarm,
        Scattering the people, as torn-up paper
        Rags and utensils in a sudden gust,
        Seized with immeasurable neurotic dread.

        Financier, leaving your little room
        Where the money is made but not spent,
        You'll need your typist and your boy no more;
        The game is up for you and for the others,
        Who, thinking, pace in slippers on the lawns
        Of College Quad or Cathedral Close,
        Who are born nurses, who live in shorts
        Sleeping with people and playing fives.
        Seekers after happiness, all who follow
        The convolutions of your simple wish,
        It is later than you think; nearer that day
        Far other than that distant afternoon

Amid rustle of frocks and stamping feet

W. H.
AUDEN

They gave the prizes to the ruined boys.
You cannot be away, then, no
Not though you pack to leave within an hour,
Escaping humming down arterial roads:
The date was yours; the prey to fugues,
Irregular breathing and alternate ascendancies
After some haunted migratory years
To disintegrate on an instant in the explosion of mania
Or lapse for ever into a classic fatigue.

'SIR, NO MAN'S ENEMY'

Sir, no man's enemy, forgiving all
But will his negative inversion, be prodigal:
Send to us power and light, a sovereign touch
Curing the intolerable neural itch,
The exhaustion of weaning, the liar's quinsy,
And the distortions of ingrown virginity.
Prohibit sharply the rehearsed response
And gradually correct the coward's stance;
Cover in time with beams those in retreat
That, spotted, they turn though the reverse were great;
Publish each healer that in city lives
Or country houses at the end of drives;
Harrow the house of the dead; look shining at
New styles of architecture, a change of heart.

'OUR HUNTING FATHERS'

Our hunting fathers told the story
    Of the sadness of the creatures,
Pitied the limits and the lack
    Set in their finished features;
Saw in the lion's intolerant look,
Behind the quarry's dying glare
Love raging for the personal glory
    That reason's gift would add,
The liberal appetite and power,
    The rightness of a god.

Who nurtured in that fine tradition
    Predicted the result,
Guessed Love by nature suited to
    The intricate ways of guilt;
That human company could so
His southern gestures modify
And make it his mature ambition
    To think no thought but ours,
To hunger, work illegally,
    And be anonymous?

A BRIDE IN THE '30'S

W. H.
AUDEN

(*For Madame Mangeot*)

Easily, my dear, you move, easily your head
And easily as through leaves of a photograph album I'm
    led
Through the night's delights and the day's impressions
Past the tall tenements and the trees in the wood
Though sombre the sixteen skies of Europe
             And the Danube flood.

Looking and loving our behaviours pass
The stones the steels and the polished glass;
Lucky to love the new pansy railway
The sterile farms where his looks are fed,
And in the policed unlucky city
             Lucky his bed.

He from these lands of terrifying mottoes
Makes worlds as innocent as Beatrix Potter's;
Through bankrupt countries where they mend the
    roads
Along the endless plains his will is
Intent as a collector to pursue
             His greens and lilies.

Easy for him to find in your face
The pool of silence and the tower of grace
To conjure a camera into a wishing rose
Simple to excite in the air from a glance
The horses, the fountains, the sidedrum, the trombone
             And the dance, the dance.

W. H. Summoned by such a music from our time
AUDEN Such images to audience come
As vanity cannot dispel nor bless:
Hunger and love in their variations
Grouped invalids watching the flight of the birds
And single assassins.

Ten thousand of the desperate marching by
Five feet, six feet, seven feet high:
Hitler and Mussolini in their wooing poses
Churchill acknowledging the voter's greeting
Roosevelt at the microphone, Van Lubbe laughing
And our first meeting.

But love except at our proposal
Will do no trick at his disposal;
Without opinions of his own performs
The programme that we think of merit,
And through our private stuff must work
His public spirit.

Certain it became while we were still incomplete
There were certain prizes for which we would never
compete;
A choice was killed by every childish illness,
The boiling tears among the hothouse plants,
The rigid promise fractured in the garden,
And the long aunts.

And every day there bolted from the field
Desires to which we could not yield;
Fewer and clearer grew the plans,
Schemes for a life and sketches for a hatred,
And early among my interesting scrawls
Appeared your portrait.

You stand now before me, flesh and bone
Are they your choices? O, be deaf
To hatred proffering immediate pleasure
Glory to swap her fascinating rubbish
                    For your one treasure.

Be deaf too standing uncertain now,
A pine tree shadow across your brow,
To what I hear and wish I did not,
The voice of love saying lightly, brightly
'Be Lubbe, Be Hitler, but be my good
                    Daily, nightly'.

The power which corrupts, that power to excess
The beautiful quite naturally possess:
To them the fathers and the children turn
And all who long for their destruction
The arrogant and self-insulted wait
                    The looked instruction.

Shall idleness ring then your eyes like the pest?
O will you unnoticed and mildly like the rest,
Will you join the lost in their sneering circles,
Forfeit the beautiful interest and fall
Where the engaging face is the face of the betrayer
                    And the pang is all?

Wind shakes the tree; the mountains darken:
And the heart repeats though we would not hearken;
'Yours the choice to whom the gods awarded
The language of learning and the language of love
Crooked to move as a moneybug or a cancer
                    Or straight as a dove'.

EPILOGUE FROM 'THE ORATORS'

'O where are you going?' said reader to rider,
'That valley is fatal when furnaces burn,
Yonder's the midden whose odours will madden,
That gap is the grave where the tall return.'

'O do you imagine', said fearer to farer,
'That dusk will delay on your path to the pass,
Your diligent looking discover the lacking
Your footsteps feel from granite to grass?'

'O what was that bird', said horror to hearer,
'Did you see that shape in the twisted trees?
Behind you swiftly the figure comes softly,
The spot on your skin is a shocking disease?'

'Out of this house'—said rider to reader
'Yours never will'—said farer to fearer
'They're looking for you'—said hearer to horror
As he left them there, as he left them there.

LOUIS MACNEICE

AN ECLOGUE FOR CHRISTMAS

A. I meet you in an evil time.

B.   The evil bells
   Put out of our heads, I think, the thought of every-
       thing else.

A. The jaded calender revolves,
   Its nuts need oil, carbon chokes the valves,
   The excess sugar of a diabetic culture
   Rotting the nerve of life and literature;
   Therefore when we bring out the old tinsel and
       frills
   To announce that Christ is born among the barbar-
       ous hills
   I turn to you whom a morose routine
   Saves from the mad vertigo of being what has been.

B. Analogue of me, you are wrong to turn to me,
   My country will not yield you any sanctuary,
   There is no pinpoint in any of the ordnance maps
   To save you when your towns and town-bred
       thoughts collapse,
   It is better to die *in situ* as I shall,
   One place is as bad as another. Go back where your
       instincts call
   And listen to the crying of the town-cats and the
       taxis again,
   Or wind your gramophone and eavesdrop on great
       men.

A. Jazz-weary of years of drums and Hawaian guitar,
Pivoting on the parquet I seem to have moved far
From bombs and mud and gas, have stuttered on my
    feet
Clinched to the streamlined and butter-smooth
    trulls of the élite,
The lights irritating and gyrating and rotating in
    gauze—
Pomade-dazzle, a slick beauty of gewgaws—
I who was Harlequin in the childhood of the
    century,
Posed by Picasso beside an endless opaque sea,
Have seen myself sifted and splintered in broken
    facets,
Tentative pencillings, endless liabilities, no assets,
Abstractions scalpelled with a palette-knife
Without reference to this particular life,
And so it has gone on; I have not been allowed to be
Myself in flesh or face, but abstracting and dissecting
    me
They have made of me pure form, a symbol or a
    pastiche,
Stylised profile, anything but soul and flesh:
And that is why I turn this jaded music on
To forswear thought and become an automaton.

B. There are in the country also of whom I am afraid—
Men who put beer into a belly that is dead,
Women in the forties with terrier and setter who
    whistle and swank
Over down and plough and Roman road and daisied
    bank,
Half-conscious that these barriers over which they
    stride

Are nothing to the barbed wire that has grown
    round their pride.

LOUIS
MAC-
NEICE

A. And two there are, as I drive in the city, who
    suddenly perturb—
  The one sirening me to draw up by the kerb
  The other, as I lean back, my right leg stretched
    creating speed,
  Making me catch and stamp, the brakes shrieking,
    pull up dead:
  She wears silk stockings taunting the winter wind,
  He carries a white stick to mark that he is blind.

B. In the country they are still hunting, in the heavy
    shires
  Greyness is on the fields and sunset like a line of
    pyres
  Of barbarous heroes smoulders through the ancient
    air
 Hazed with factory dust and, orange opposite, the
    moon's glare,
  Goggling yokel-stubborn through the iron trees,
  Jeers at the end of us, our bland ancestral ease;
  We shall go down like palaeolithic man
  Before some new Ice Age or Genghiz Khan.

A. It is time for some new coinage, people have got so
    old,
  Hacked and handled and shiny from pocketing they
    have made bold
  To think that each is himself through these
    accidents, being blind
  To the fact that they are merely the counters of an
    unknown Mind.

A Mind that does not think, if such a thing can be,
Mechanical Reason, capricious Identity.
That I could be able to face this domination nor
    flinch—

A. The tin toys of the hawker move on the pavement
    inch by inch
Not knowing that they are wound up; it is better to
    be so
Than to be, like us, wound up and while running
    down to know—

B. But everywhere the pretence of individuality
    recurs—

A. Old faces frosted with powder and choked in furs.

B. The jutlipped farmer gazing over the humpbacked
    wall.

A. The commercial traveller joking in the urinal.

B. I think things draw to an end, the soil is stale.

A. And over-elaboration will nothing now avail,
The street is up again, gas, electricity or drains,
Ever-changing conveniences, nothing comfortable
    remains
Un-improved, as flagging Rome improved villa and
    sewer
(A sound-proof library and a stable temperature).
Our street is up, red lights sullenly mark
The long trench of pipes, iron guts in the dark,
And not till the Goths again come swarming down
    the hill
Will cease the clangour of the electric drill.
But yet there is beauty narcotic and deciduous
In this vast organism grown out of us:

On all the traffic islands stand white globes like   LOUIS
    moons,   MAC-
The city's haze is clouded amber that purrs and   NEICE
    croons,
And tilting by the noble curve bus after tall bus
    comes
With an osculation of yellow light, with a glory like
    chrysanthemums.

B. The country gentry cannot change, they will die in
    their shoes
From angry circumstance and moral self-abuse,
Dying with a paltry fizzle they will prove their lives
    to be
An ever-diluted drug, a spiritual tautology.
They cannot live once their idols are turned out,
None of them can endure, for how could they,
    possibly, without
The flotsam of private property, pekingese and
    polyanthus,
The good things which in the end turn to poison
    and pus,
Without the bandy chairs and the sugar in the silver
    tongs
And the inter-ripple and resonance of years of
    dinner-gongs?
Or if they could find no more that cumulative proof
In the rain dripping off the conservatory roof?
What will happen when the only sanction the
    country-dweller has—

A. What will happen to us, planked and panelled with
    jazz?
Who go to the theatre where a black man dances
    like an eel,

Where pink thighs flash like the spokes of a wheel,
where we feel
That we know in advance all the jogtrot and the cake-
walk jokes,
All the bumfun and the gags of the comedians in
boaters and toques,
All the tricks of the virtuosos who invert the
usual—

B. What will happen to us when the State takes down
the manor wall,
When there is no more private shooting or fishing,
when the trees are all cut down,
When faces are all dials and cannot smile or
frown—

A. What will happen when the sniggering machine-
guns in the hands of the young men
Are trained on every flat and club and beauty
parlour and Father's den?
What will happen when our civilisation like a long
pent balloon—

B. What will happen will happen; the whore and the
buffoon
Will come off best; no dreamers, they cannot lose
their dream
And are at least likely to be reinstated in the new
régime.
But one thing is not likely—

A.   Do not gloat over yourself
Do not be your own vulture, high on some
mountain shelf
Huddle the pitiless abstractions bald about the neck

Who will descend when you crumple in the plains
    a wreck.
Over the randy of the theatre and cinema I hear
    songs
Unlike anything—

B.   The lady of the house poises the silver tongs
    And picks a lump of sugar, 'ne plus ultra' she says
    'I cannot do otherwise, even to prolong my days'—

A. I cannot do otherwise either, tonight I will book
      my seat—

B. I will walk about the farm-yard which is replete
    As with the smell of dung so with memories—

A. I will gorge myself to satiety with the oddities
    Of every artiste, official or amateur,
    Who has pleased me in my rôle of hero-worshipper
    Who has pleased me in my rôle of individual man—

B. Let us lie once more, say 'What we think, we can'
    The old idealist lie—

A.   And for me before I die
    Let me go the round of the garish glare—

B.   And on the bare and high
    Places of England, the Wiltshire Downs and the
      Long Mynd
    Let the balls of my feet bounce on the turf, my face
      burn in the wind
    My eyelashes stinging in the wind, and the sheep
      like grey stones
    Humble my human pretensions—

A.   Let the saxophones and the xylophones
    And the cult of every technical excellence, the
      miles of canvas in the galleries

And the canvas of the rich man's yacht snapping and
    tacking on the seas
And the perfection of a grilled steak—

B.   Let all these so ephemeral things
Be somehow permanent like the swallow's tangent
    wings:
Goodbye to you, this day remember is Christmas,
    this morn
They say, interpret it your own way, Christ is born.

SUNDAY MORNING

Down the road someone is practising scales,
The notes like little fishes vanish with a wink of tails,
Man's heart expands to tinker with his car
For this is Sunday morning, Fate's great bazaar,
Regard these means as ends, concentrate on this Now,
And you may grow to music or drive beyond Hindhead
    anyhow,
Take corners on two wheels until you go so fast
That you can clutch a fringe or two of the windy past,
That you can abstract this day and make it to the week
    of time
A small eternity, a sonnet self-contained in rhyme.

But listen, up the road, something gulps, the church
    spire
Opens its eight bells out, skulls' mouths which will not
    tire
To tell how there is no music or movement which
    secures
Escape from the weekday time. Which deadens and
    endures.

PERSEUS

LOUIS
MAC-
NEICE

Borrowed wings on his ankles,
Carrying a stone death,
The hero entered the hall,
All in the hall looked up,
Their breath frozen on them,
And there was no more shuffle or clatter in the hall at all.

So a friend of a man comes in
And leaves a book he is lending or flowers
And goes again, alive but as good as dead,
And you are left alive, no better than dead,
And you dare not turn the leaden pages of the book or
    touch the flowers, the hooded and arrested hours.

Shut your eyes,
There are suns beneath your lids,
Or look in the looking-glass in the end room—
You will find it full of eyes,
The ancient smiles of men cut out with scissors and
    kept in mirrors.

Ever to meet me comes, in sun or dull,
The gay hero swinging the Gorgon's head
And I am left, with the dull drumming of the sun,
    suspended and dead,
Or the dumb grey-brown of the day is a leper's cloth,
And one feels the earth going round and round the
    globe of the blackening mantle, a mad moth.

THE CREDITOR

The quietude of a soft wind
Will not rescind
My debts to God, but gentle-skinned
His finger probes. I lull myself
In quiet in diet in riot in dreams,
In dopes in drams in drums in dreams
Till God retire and the door shut.
But
Now I am left in the fire-blaze
The peacefulness of the fire-blaze
Will not erase
My debts to God for his mind strays
Over and under and all ways
All days and always.

SNOW

The room was suddenly rich and the great bay-
    window was
Spawning snow and pink roses against it
Soundlessly collateral and incompatible:
World is suddener than we fancy it.

World is crazier and more of it than we think,
Incorrigibly plural. I peel and portion
A tangerine and spit the pips and feel
The drunkenness of things being various.

And the fire flames with a bubbling sound for world
Is more spiteful and gay than one supposes—
On the tongue on the eyes on the ears in the palms of
    one's hands—
There is more than glass between the snow and the
    huge roses.

STEPHEN SPENDER

THE PRISONERS

Far far the least of all, in want,
Are these,
The prisoners
Turned massive with their vaults and dark with dark.

They raise no hands, which rest upon their knees,
But lean their solid eyes against the night,
Dimly they feel
Only the furniture they use in cells.

Their Time is almost Death. The silted flow
Of years on years
Is marked by dawns
As faint as cracks on mud-flats of despair.

My pity moves amongst them like a breeze
On walls of stone
Fretting for summer leaves, or like a tune
On ears of stone.

Then, when I raise my hands to strike,
It is too late,
There are no chains that fall
Nor visionary liquid door
Melted with anger.

When have their lives been free from walls and dark
And airs that choke?
And where less prisoner to let my anger
Like a sun strike?

STEPHEN
SPENDER If I could follow them from room to womb
To plant some hope
Through the black silk of the big-bellied gown
There would I win.

No, no, no,
It is too late for anger,
Nothing prevails
But pity for the grief they cannot feel.

'IN RAILWAY HALLS'

In railway halls, on pavements near the traffic,
They beg, their eyes made big by empty staring
And only measuring Time, like the blank clock.

No, I shall weave no tracery of pen-ornament
To make them birds upon my singing-tree:
Time merely drives these lives which do not live
As tides push rotten stuff along the shore.

—There is no consolation, no, none
In the curving beauty of that line
Traced on our graphs through history, where the
       oppressor
Starves and deprives the poor.

Paint here no draped despairs, no saddening clouds
Where the soul rests, proclaims eternity.
But let the wrong cry out as raw as wounds
This Time forgets and never heals, far less transcends.

'NOT PALACES, AN ERA'S CROWN'

STEPHEN
SPENDER

Not palaces, an era's crown
Where the mind dwells, intrigues, rests;
The architectural gold-leaved flower
From people ordered like a single mind,
I build. This only what I tell:
It is too late for rare accumulation
For family pride, for beauty's filtered dusts;
I say, stamping the words with emphasis,
Drink from here energy and only energy,
As from the electric charge of a battery,
To will this Time's change.
Eye, gazelle, delicate wanderer,
Drinker of horizon's fluid line;
Ear that suspends on a chord
The spirit drinking timelessness;
Touch, love, all senses;
Leave your gardens, your singing feasts,
Your dreams of suns circling before our sun,
Of heaven after our world.
Instead, watch images of flashing brass
That strike the outward sense, the polished will
Flag of our purpose which the wind engraves.
No spirit seek here rest. But this: No man
Shall hunger: Man shall spend equally.
Our goal which we compel: Man shall be man.

—That programme of the antique Satan
Bristling with guns on the indented page
With battleship towering from hilly waves:
For what? Drive of a ruining purpose
Destroying all but its age-long exploiters.
Our programme like this, yet opposite,
Death to the killers, bringing light to life.

'AFTER THEY HAVE TIRED'

After they have tired of the brilliance of cities
And of striving for office where at last they may
      languish
Hung round with easy chains until
Death and Jerusalem glorify also the crossing-sweeper:
Then those streets the rich built and their easy love
Fade like old cloths, and it is death stalks through life
Grinning white through all faces
Clean and equal like the shine from snow.

In this time when grief pours freezing over us,
When the hard light of pain gleams at every street
      corner,
When those who were pillars of that day's gold roof
Shrink in their clothes; surely from hunger
We may strike fire, like fire from flint?
And our strength is now the strength of our bones
Clean and equal like the shine from snow
And the strength of famine and of our enforced idle-
      ness,
And it is the strength of our love for each other.

Readers of this strange language,
We have come at last to a country
Where light equal, like the shine from snow, strikes all
      faces,
Here you may wonder
How it was that works, money, interest, building,
      could ever hide
The palpable and obvious love of man for man.

Oh comrades, let not those who follow after
—The beautiful generation that shall spring from our
      sides—

Let not them wonder how after the failure of banks
The failure of cathedrals and the declared insanity of
    our rulers,
We lacked the Spring-like resources of the tiger
Or of plants who strike out new roots to gushing
    waters.
But through torn-down portions of old fabric let their
    eyes
Watch the admiring dawn explode like a shell
Around us, dazing us with light like snow.

THE NORTH

Our single purpose was to walk through snow
With faces swung to their prodigious North
Like compass iron. As clerks in whited Banks
With bird-claw pens column virgin paper
To snow we added footprints.
Extensive whiteness drowned
All sense of space. We tramped through
Static, glaring days, Time's suspended blank.
That was in Spring and Autumn. Then Summer struck
Water over rocks, and half the world
Became a ship with a deep keel, the booming floes
And icebergs with their little birds.
Twittering Snow Bunting, Greenland Wheatear
Red throated Divers; imagine butterflies
Sulphurous cloudy yellow; glory of bees
That suck from saxifrage; crowberry,
Bilberry, cranberry, *Pyrola uniflora*.
There followed winter in a frozen hut
Warm enough at the kernel, but dare to sleep

STEPHEN With head against the wall—ice gummed my hair.
SPENDER Hate Culver's loud breathing, despise Freeman's
Fidget for washing; love only the dogs
That whine for scraps and scratch. Notice
How they run better (on short journeys) with a bitch.
In that, different from us.

Return, return, you warn. We do. There is
A network of railways, money, words, words, words.
Meals, papers, exchanges, debates,
Cinema, wireless; the worst is Marriage.
We cannot sleep. At night we watch
A speaking clearness through cloudy paranoia.
These questions are white rifts. Was
Ice our anger transformed? The raw, the motionless
Skies, were these the spirit's hunger?
The continual and hypnotized march through snow
The dropping nights of precious extinction, were these
Only the wide invention of the will,
The frozen will's evasion? If this exists
In us as madness here, as coldness
In these summer, civilized sheets: is the North
Over there, a tangible real madness
A glittering simpleton, one without towns
Only with bears and fish, a staring eye,
A new and singular sex?

AN ELEMENTARY SCHOOL CLASSROOM

Far far from gusty waves, these children's faces
Like rootless weeds the torn hair round their paleness;
The tall girl with her weighed-down head; the paper-
seeming boy with rat's eyes; the stunted unlucky heir
Of twisted bones, reciting a father's gnarled disease,

His lesson from his desk. At back of the dim class
One unnoted, mild and young: his eyes live in a dream
Of squirrel's game, in tree room, other than this.

On sour cream walls, donations; Shakespeare's head
Cloudless at dawn, civilized dome riding all cities;
Belled, flowery, Tyrolese valley; open-handed map
Awarding the explicit world, of every name but here.
To few, too few, these are real windows: world and
          words and waving
Leaves, to heal. For these young lives, guilty and
          dangerous
Is fantasy of travel. Surely, Shakespeare is wicked

To lives that wryly turn, under the structural Lie,
Toward smiles or hate? Amongst their heap, these
          children
Wear skins peeped through by bones, and spectacles of
          steel
With mended glass, like bottle bits in slag.
Tyrol is wicked; map's promising a fable:
All of their time and space are foggy slum,
So blot their maps with slums as big as doom.

Unless, dowager, governor, these pictures, in a room
Columned above childishness, like our day's future
          drift
Of smoke concealing war, are voices shouting
O that beauty has words and works which break
Through coloured walls and towers. The children
          stand
As in a climbing mountain train. This lesson illustrates
The world green in their many valleys beneath:
The total summer heavy with their flowers.

THE EXILES

History has tongues
Has angels has guns—has saved has praised—
Today proclaims
Achievements of her exiles long returned,
Now no more rootless, for whom her printing
Glazes their bruised waste years with one
Balancing present presented sky.

Hold the achievement, how her men like flags
Unfurled upon her shore are cupped by waves:
The laurelled exiles, kissing own sands and shells.

Number there freedom's friends. One who
Within the element of endless summer
Like leaf in amber, petrified by sun,
Studied the root of action. Some, in cafés,
Endured the drowning flakes of stranger tongues.
Also a poet was babbling like a fountain
Through Twickenham Garden. Now, all these
Drink their just light from cups.

Their deeds and deaths are birds. They stop the invisible
Speed of our empty sight across the past.
In our eyes' pigment these feed and fly and dwell.

Their time and land are death; since all
States and stays and makes
Them one with what they willed. Now we endure
Perennial unseasonableness, waiting
For that death. Our life's the metal
That welds complexity of actual being
To those lucid deaths preceding. We, waiting, till
The signatory laurel's single green
Shall flash our hungered lives with leaves
Of justification.

Yet in the accomplishment
Of those exiles returned—where
Is their wandering fearful knee? In the assertion
Of glossing paper sky, where does the blemish
Of sexual despair speck the clear dome
With an ape's venery? How shall these severed lives
Of spirit's hunger, spite's malaria
—The hate-planted tree—o dissolve and re-form
To a rosy finger's touch of history our creator?

History has tongues
Has angels has guns—has saved has praised—
The veins
That travel through the brain, no longer croak
Hunger and headache: they become
Taut wires that lift a dance of words
Across a desert. The exiled dead,
Not ghosts, but winning messages, return, return.

THE UNCREATING CHAOS

I

To the hanging despair of eyes in the street, offer
Your making hands and your guts on skewers of pity.
When the thunder sky is built with clouds like sand,
      which the yellow
Sun trumpets above, respond to that day's shrillness
With a headache. Like a ghost, follow, follow
The young men to the Pole, up Everest, to war: by
      love, be shot.

*   *   *

For the uncreating chaos descends
And claims you in marriage: though a man, you were
      ever a bride:

STEPHEN Ever beneath the supple surface of summer muscle,
SPENDER The evening talk like fountains cupping the summer
          stars,
The friend who chucked back the lock from his brow
          in front of a glass,
You were only anxious that all these loves would last.
Your primal mover anxiety
Was a grave lecher, a globe-trotter, one
Whose moods were straws, the winds that puffed
          them, aeroplanes.
'Whatever happens, I shall never be alone
 Ishall always have a boy, a railway fare, or a revolution.'

          *   *   *

Without your buttressing gesture that yet so leans;
Is glad as a mat
When stamped on; blood that cries to give suck to a bat;
And your heart fretted by winds like rocks at Britain's
          end;
You would stand alone in a silence that never uttered,
And stare in yourself as though on a desolate room.

II

Supposing then you change
Gestures, clamp your mind in irons,
By boxed degrees transform into past history:
Stand on the astringent self-created promontory,
A Greek as simple as a water clock,
And let the traffic creak beneath.
You'd live then in the tricks of dreams, you'd be
Not living, but a walking wish, private and malicious
As my cracked aunt, or if blown, like a banker.

          *   *   *

I will confess to you
At night I'm flooded by my conscious future,

The bursting tide of an unharnessed power
That drowns my will of now.
In thoughts where pity is the same as cruelty
I dream of you as water. Whether
What flows and wavers is my self
Or my thought streaming over you—or upon all
The town and time—we are the same.
And outside are the speed bikes' hundred mile an hour
Snorting in circles on their plain: the riders lose
All sense of time and place: they're ridden by
Their speed: the men are the machines.

    *   *   *

All I can warn today—more I shall learn—
Is that our fear makes being migratory.
Shall falsify your peace into a soldier:
Shall coin you into savage when you flee
The terrible crystal civilization dangles:
Shall make you choose a lover like a mirror
Inventing and reflecting gunmen in you.
You are a ghost amongst the flares of guns,
Less living than
The shattered dead whose veins of mineral
We mine for here.
      Alter your life.

III

Dissection of Empires, multiplication of crowns
By secret treaty. But the pigeons scatter
From sunlit pavement at the fatal shot.
Crowns and heads bounce like hoops down stone steps.

    *   *   *

Meagre men shoot up. Like Verey Light
A corporal's wagging tongue burns above burning
   parliament.

STEPHEN There flows in the tide of killers, the whip masters,
SPENDER Breeches and gaiters camouflage blood,
Gangsters shooting from hips, pathics with rubber
truncheons,
Spontaneous joy in the padded cell.

*   *   *

Centrifugal movements of a will
Invent these violent patterns.
History rushes. The crowds in towns,
Cerebral boundaries of nations over mountains,
Actors in flesh and death and material nature,
Dance to a gripless private stammer of shouting,
Like thoughts in a minister's dying brain.

*   *   *

Shall I never reach
The field guarded by stones
Precious in the stone mountains,
Where the scytheless wind
Flushes the warm grasses:
Where clouds without rain
Add to the sun
With their lucid sailing shine?
The simple mechanism is here
Clear day, thoughts of the table, the desk,
The hand, symbols of power.
Here the veins may pour
Into the deed, as the field
Into the standing corn.
Meanwhile, where nothing's pious
And life no longer willed
Nor the human will conscious,
Holy is lucidity
And the mind that dare explain.

JAMES REEVES

THE HOUR AND THE STORM

Summer for England ends: simple and likeable
This moving a clock's hands, as if saying
'With this act we cancel formally the summer;
We'll have no lingering last-rose last-post sweetness
Of breath-moist bugle flowering in the dusk.
Winterwards turn we the face of time.'

The Hour bows over me,
Her eyes under the unfalling lashes
Are unreproachful and unbargaining:
She whom I always tried to elbow out
And cried against, this creature summons me
With how indifferent an imperiousness.
Useless to shield the face from that command.
Cry now, faint Human—nothing to cry unless
'Mercifully stifle with your fast embrace
This pitiful quivered protest or that shame,
Hour, blot out the tremulous mouth
That stills itself upon your heartlessness.'

In the country early darkness brings the trees closer.
Walking homeward I feel them bending over me.
The fallen leaves startle my feet.
I hurry on for letters and late tea.
Soon the ground-mist covers the dying leaves.

The Storm protests the Hour:
But too wild a tattered breast to nestle in.
Only the wind supports; that bitter staff
None falls with though he cry

JAMES 'Fall, wind, that I may fall.' His cries—
REEVES Anguish of unknown revelling, writhed rags of starved
        rebellion—
      Tear from him, whirl with leaves, the flayed trees
      Sob and shudder amidst the whelming rage.

      O leaves, that the sun's fire fingered
      And the loves of birds fêted, their music multiplied,
      Wind-patterned endlessly against that blue
      And sped along the idle stream
      Where fish the frolic spun through fretted shallows:
      Are you remembered of the sapless trees—
      Their summer habit? do you remember
      Playing in the sun? and playing was deceit?

      Hour, who are the Hour found again,
      After the Storm's stolen interval,
      Waiting, unblown, more merciless,
      Will you forgive me if I say
      'I am not less than trees divided
      Between calm and wildness,
      Smooth-falling leaves and heart like weather
      Raging with the wind when comes
      The Storm to voice hushed cries of fate.'

CLIMBING A MOUNTAIN

JAMES
REEVES

'Addío!' 'Addío!' The guide and the guide's wife
Tenderly, in the warm hut before dawn,
Parted after the breakfast by lamplight;
And I went on, down the little path over the stream;
The guide came with the rope and the other things
And led the way up silently between the fir-trees.

Up and up, on dogged metal my feet carried me,
Toward the distant shoulder; above it hung
The watery and foreboding moon, fading.
In my eyes was the grey light
And the guide pointing to signs of the War,
Brutal, jagged wire and tumble-down dugouts:
In my heart—but I did not know where my heart was,
Or why the rocks above me seemed more brutal,
Or my feet glad, carrying me up, out of the valley.

Dawn was above us, creeping down the white summit,
But we still were in twilight. I heard,
Under the scrunch of my feet across the gravel,
The stream's quick broken tumbling in the valley.
At last we reached the snow, and stopped. It was very
     lonely.
The guide undid his rucksack, saying something gay,
And we rigged ourselves out for crossing the snowfield.

I felt good in my legs, all dressed up like a Russian;
But my heart hadn't come with me—I knew that now,
Panting and stumbling. I had no competence,
I felt feeble and small after a while
As I struggled up behind the mountaineer.

We had to keep stopping, I was so weary.
A little wind would blow over the desolate snowfield
And the guide would breathe it; it was his breath.

JAMES When we came to rock again, it was the same:
REEVES He would look between rocks, down, down
Into the stony heart of the mountain,
And that would be his heart and the mountain-sides his
    sides.

When the wind dropped on the snowfield I would hear
The little stream bumping away in the valley,
And that would be my heart, I thought.
'Must you drone there always,' I said, 'will-less and
    idle?
Come up and help me, skulker in the depth!
My legs are faint now, my blood is without ambition.'
And my heart mumbled and became inaudible.

'Very well,' I thought, 'I will go without you.'
And on we went; we kicked our way out of the snow
And began to ascend over the rock. By this time
The dawn had been swallowed up in a moist haze.
Soon I was quite without pride, and the climber's
    emulation;
I let the guide haul me up over the difficult bits;
I didn't care what he thought of me,
I didn't want to get to the top—
Except that it was probably the quickest way down
    now!

I was glad when I stumbled off the rock
And stood on the edge of the snow plateau.
The guide looked at the snow and back at the rock
And he loved them both with his eyes,
Like a child caressing its own innocent flesh.
Then, as we went on across the last level,
There seemed nothing to breathe; I was unconscious;
And there was nothing to see either, except the snow

Sodden with mist, and yielding; leprous it seemed.

At the summit there was a book in a metal box.
We sat down and wrote in it solemnly.
I didn't look at the guide. I looked round me into the
    mist.
We took out our food. He gave me some red wine
    from his flask.
As he did so the flask clinked on the cup,
Hollow and dead in the rare, muffled quiet.
At last he spoke, slowly, in his soft clinging tongue—
A sort of congratulation, and something sad about the
    weather.

Well, this was the top. In a way I was proud,
Though I'd nothing to be proud of, a failure in achieve-
    ment.
I had lost my self, my heart, where the guide had
    found his.
My heart was down there all the time,
Perhaps now in the Albergo, singing songs and drink-
    ing,
And laughing at the Italian tourists
(The little heads and the big chests)
Who buccaneered through their stolen country in
    shiny cars,
And the German tourists who came to gather plants.

But wasn't it good, my heart, to leave you for a while?
Wasn't it good, for a few hours, to wrench myself
Out of the sun's embrace, the indolent valley,
To spurn you, to be alone, to be comfortless?
Yes, churlish heart, it was good: to be lost
These long stolen hours from you—
First and most fulsome of counsellors.

JAMES
REEVES

AT THE WINDOW

Then more-than-morning quiet
The pretty lawn extended;
And rooted trees stood tall
On westward shadows pointing.

Answering no will my hand
Dropped from the window catch,
My throat to know faltered
Whether sob or sing.

Why trees were not, nor morning,
No flash of mind revealed;
Maybe throat found and hands met
A memory more clear than sight.

CHARLES MADGE

BLOCKING THE PASS

With an effort Grant swung the great block,
The swivel operated and five or six men
Crouched under the lee of the straight rock.

They waited in silence or counting ten,
They thrust their fingers in their wet hair,
The steel sweated in their hands. And then

The clouds hurried across a sky quite bare,
The sounds of the station, three miles off, ceased,
The dusty birds hopped keeping watch. And there

Arose to what seemed as high as the sky at least,
Arose a giant and began to die,
Arose such a shape as the night in the East.

The stones sobbed, the trees gave a cry,
A tremulous wonder shook animal and plant,
And a decapitating anger stirred the sky

And alone, on a tall stone, stood Grant.

FORTUNE

The natural silence of a tree,
The motion of a mast upon the fresh-tossing sea,
Now foam-inclined, now to the sun with dignity,

Or the stone brow of a mountain
Regarded from a town, or the curvet-fountain,
Or one street-stopped in wonder at the fountain,

Or a great cloud entering the room of the sky,
Napoleon of his century,
Heard come to knowing music consciously,

Such, not us, reflect and have their day,
We are but vapour of today
Unless love's chance fall on us and call us away

As the wind takes what it can
And blowing on the fortunate face, reveals the man.

LOSS

Like the dark germs across the filter clean
So in the clear day of a thousand years
This dusty cloud is creeping to our eyes,

Here, as we grow, and are as we have been
Or living give for life some morning tears
The flowering hour bent and unconscious lies.

As in Vienna now, the wounded walls
Silently speak, as deep in Austria
The battered shape of man is without shade

So, time in metaphor, tomorrow falls
On Europe, Asia and America,
And houses vanish, even as they were made,

For yesterday is always sad, its nature
Darker than love would wish in every feature.

SOLAR CREATION

CHARLES
MADGE

The sun, of whose terrain we creatures are,
Is the director of all human love,
Unit of time, and circle round the earth,

And we are the commotion born of love
And slanted rays of that illustrious star,
Peregrine of the crowded fields of birth,

The crowded lane, the market and the tower.
Like sight in pictures, real at remove,
Such is our motion on dimensional earth.

Down by the river, where the ragged are,
Continuous the cries and noise of birth,
While to the muddy edge dark fishes move,

And over all, like death, or sloping hill,
Is nature, which is larger and more still.

AT WAR

Fire rides calmly in the air
That blows across the fields of water
That laps the papped curve of the outspread earth.

Earth is bone and builds the house
Water the blood that softly runs inside
Air is the breath by which the fire is fed.

Earth's mouth is open and will suck you down
Water climbs over earth to reach you
The assassin air is at your throat
And fire will presently split the air.

THE HOURS OF THE PLANETS

☉

The summoning sun, the sun that looks on London
See twice, sees London and unLondon sees
And leaves the sound unsounded of the leafless sky.

The rise of the   Rising along the sun's long escalier
bourgeoisie.   All equal all in inequality
Looking not one to one but each from each
Different in self-indifference.

At top of steps, some half-mile from the sea
Sat—in the morning and out of the sea up to him
Came—seeking favour and on left and right
Stood——quick as trees, then said—
These are ours and therein all that is
And the living creatures of the field and fen
Made echo sound upon the day's platface.

The little fronds, the waving sleeve and skirt
Who quickly turn aside, the animals
Of sleek two-globed marble without heart,
Stones within the middle of their eyes,
They know not what they feel.
                                    Save passion for them.

The sun from his hauteur inclines
Upon the various crops and
The tiger hinterland. The forests of daylight.

The sun stat. And looking back
Down back upon in ewig retrograde.

♀

The little sun fled backward through the sky
The airy cloudy cumulus split every way
The remote sea was with the remote fish.

Merciless into morsels
She cut her young brother and cast them
On the sea where each a battleship became
In whitest blossom decked.

*The memories
of the past
become the
images of the
present.*

The whole of London was a sea of lilies.
The captain said who stood upon the bridge
That is Absyrt.

There came a storm. The tallest cruiser
Heaven's finger touched unfolded in ros flame.

'there is no way to restore life'

*Inward
monitions:*

'glaze the dark eye that holds eternity'

The towers came nearer over the mist.
I heard my kind pattering all about
The shafts, the upward and the downward shafts,
And rolling silent out in silent daylight
Innumerous pellicules.
                    Passed the X
And cliff of many windows, slept along
Crossed by the Pass of two Towers
And so ad infinitum to the stars.

*Glimpses of
reality.*

☿

The sun will press his hands over my eyes
Coming unawares.

*The future
comes.*

The silent groups are scattered in the fields
No talk goes up from them, they wave like trees.

*Youth on the
approach of
age.*

319

CHARLES There will murmur as the spirits move
MADGE Two from this quarter yonder unperceived.

The ancient clocks look down
Thereupon the wise drawn into corners
Unhollow their rigid countenances.

Telegraphy Flowing quickly, quietly wisdom will be
and Killing by distance the great idiot sky.
human
generation. They wave, they falter, sisters and daughters
On the wave their motion pauses, falls, is free.

Water leaps from naked rock unafraid
Swift in twisting a garland and a smile.

Nature as the Two wanderers that were in a month
unity of Heard a cry, Oh mother I shall die
contraries. Then secretly was born
The father of death and healing
The day grew cold and still
As the embrace of enemies at war
Upon a mountain rich with copper ore.

☾

MAN MANIFORM

Real houses, real inhabitants—
One hears them coming up the daylight street
And turning into men, extraordinary,
Familiar as two hands or constant care.
The throng whose noise is always heard outside
Whose tongues are in their heels upon the stones.
In images they seem to cross a bridge
The via media of living and dead,
Thames representing their unconsciousness.

Life, more persistent than thought, continues to flow   CHARLES
Out of Europe grown gaunt and old   MADGE
Multiple genera untabulated
Carrying pouches, tufted behind ears,
Splay-footed, hammer-fingered, hooked, humped
The smooth, the rough, the freckled and the white,
The denizens of holes, the desert prowlers,
Moon-sprung, sun-hatched, dense aground, lone up
     high,
Ragged swamp dwellers, perchers in tiptops,
Insignia, plumes, bandages, clothes, flowers,
Beautifully wrapped simple forms of life;
The growing leaves are wet with primal tears
In middlesex the semi-animal kingdom.

O reich of riches, urbs of all superb
When will you break your banks? The vague of water
Is everywhere afar and every weir
Life likening to its opponent, and susurrus
Of the grey-haired waterfall.

Deep in the water eye have gazing seen
A drowned second sun, like a dissected heart.

ℏ

Now English eyes the cancerous sun behold!   *The future of*
Bright over blackened Africa, Sahara   *mankind.*
Futurity and all paluster lakes of sewage,
Utter blackness, uttering thundercloud
On native waste and villages of hut
Far as I can see
Earth's declivity is infinite
Falling away, fading in infinite forms
Horizon added to horizon.

CHARLES Man stands black within the pause of thought
MADGE Shadowless perpendicular under beam
In deafmute equatorial solitude
When Fulmen falls, resounds among remaining
      mountains.

Then might you hear like birds between
The knocking together of love sighs
Such meditation of self-gazing self
And smooth as day-divided time
A careless phantom rapture

FAR FROM THE SUN
FARTHER FROM THE SUN
FARTHEST FROM THE SUN

DEEP IN THE EARTH
DEEPER IN THE EARTH
DEEPEST IN THE EARTH

THE DREAM WILL BEGIN
THE DREAM IS BEGINNING
THE DREAM HAS BEGUN

THREE EARS OF CORN IN A SATURNIAN
      FIELD
THREE STEAMERS ANCHORED IN A
      NEPTUNIAN SEA
THREE SOARING SPIRES IN A URANIAN SKY

Ever they change, spires steamers ears of corn,
Ages of gloomy iron, ages of stone
And golden ages that return anew
In shadows of the darksome working man
Transmuted by the secret stone of life
No stone, the lost identity of change.

The trees expand, the chestnut floribund
Spreads ever huger, and the passers by
Melt one by one into the distant air.

CHARLES
MADGE

2⟁

SCENE

A coloured page, a coloured piece of glass
A reverie, a picture of a man
An element, a wand, a wandering mind

CHARACTERS

Those who plough the hollow cave
And reap the breeze

Those who rule the sky
Dividing as they will in wives and children
Plying the compasses of golden art

The brothers of earth, sea and air
And the immortal sisters who inspire
The wakeful

THE KEY

Read backwards.
                          Leaf by leaf
Let them fall profuse and glorious
The spectrum of the interlinear eye,
In the celestial field, the cloth of gold.
Turn backwards into white prehistory
Towards the invisible cisalpine skull.
Here pause, and look upon the title page.

♂

It is today, when silence falls,
And all the people standing on the quay
To watch the big ship sail away
Stop waving to their friends
                        and say
The answer to the sun is death.

IN CONJUNCTION

Now in the circulating torrent of the stars
Certain events are drawn correct and clear
That wear expressions of anguish and delight

Signs unmistakeable of the heavenly progress
The flying planet leaves the night-house
The twined figures fill the highest hemisphere

From which we conclude peace, and grateful offerings
While the bird of war, thunderless on leaden roof
No shadow shows on the galactic brilliance of the
      streaming breast

And beyond the fated, tragic, foursquare, immovable
      house
Evenings under the trees of calm, descending evenings
      of rest
Relenting over battlefields, evenings upholding us
Among alarms, rust and the dead, waiting to be blest.

LUSTY JUVENTUS

CHARLES
MADGE

The sea is an acre of dull glass, the land is a table
My eyes jump down from the table and go running
    down as far as they are able
While one is still young and still able to employ
Nerves muscles sinews eyes mouth teeth head
A giant that threw a stone at Cærodunum
Transforming England into a salty pancake
Lichen-alive governed in gametosporous colonies
Crescented with calciform corollæ, a great stone
    marsh
With the dragons of dead Hercules debating
There is no end there is no end to the labours of
    Hercules
While one is still young and still able to employ
Feet fist eyes in the head a spade a spanner
Down down we go down the emblematic abyss
Adorned with the kisses of the gentry, come out on
    primrose day
To greet the Young Bolshevik Bolus rolling up with
    banners
Across the passes of snake and ladder country
Idly I flung down pieces, but the fit is ended
When one was wery young and able to employ
The empty salads of English advent and the formulæ of
    seajoy.

A MONUMENT

All moves within the visual frame
All walks upon the ground or stands
Casting a shadow,

All grass, day's eye, the folded man
Suffer or wither up in stone
And stare there.

They call upon the end of the world
And the last waters overwhelming
To wash the unborn things

Bedded on time's distracted coast
Bald stones and smiling silences,
Severed, they shrink.

The hovering certainty of death
Unites the water and the sky,
Their small choice

Of evils on the watching shore.

GEORGE BARKER

VERSES FOR A NURSERY WALL

The cat and the mouse
Fear the rat and fear
The man with the hat
And the house and spear,

Ladies in bright bedrooms
    Spread with glassware
    Dread the stare
    Which cannot but pass
Through twentyfive rooms
And redden the womb
And with a dark laugh
    Shatter the glassware—

Cats and ladies, wombs and glasses
Hide behind something when a man passes;
    When a man passes
    Twentyfive
    Before a man passes
    Twentyfive
Count the amount of you left alive
Be as busy as bees in a b beehive
Hide behind me the young man cried.

GEORGE
BARKER

DAEDALUS

I

Like the enormous liner of his limbs
and fell.
                    Remain behind, look on
What's left of what was once in blighted remains.
That imponderable body
                    Smote my desire, now smitten
Mortally.
                    I lift his head, his death dampens
The moist palm of my hand like handled fear
Like fear cramping my hand
and stand.
                    Remain behind, entertain posthumous fear.
I entertained.

II

Come where no crowds can trouble us divert us
No acrobats no hawkers bottles or street musicians
No towering necks like buildings overlook
Intimate revelation.

I take your hand
Spectre
And steadily lead you
Across morning haunted lawns in earlier
Days, and show
With a reversal of our growing older
How it began, what caused, the germ of time.

Where florid in the night pregnant nightdresses
Proceed sedately down unlighted stairs
Like people. And in the garden
Large lakes unreal. Hark, I hear visitant
Swans, and the moths in the trees

Like minor caverns humming. There he draws
Antennae from paralysed spiders, weapons
In his warlock fingers brandished: or runs
Engendering the eventual major strength like engines
Preparant. I cannot discern you in the leaves or in the
Undergrowth, when staring down the steep hills
He flies precipitate: Spectre. Spectre, where
If among these early places lie you, do you lie?

He fell, not then. Recently sure has fallen from that
    high
Platform. Formed in fearlessness, has fallen
Like through thought's clouds through fear, as You
    stood
Waiting with wanting breast to catch, he in his fall
Evaded. Passed towards a grave straight through.
Of Course You Knew, for saw his comet face
Approaching downward like irresistible.
I mourn him. Him I mourn, from morn to morning.

III

Where once he trod
    I cannot tread;
From the home he is gone from
    I am prohibited:
We cannot be
    While he is gone from being;
While he is not with being
    I am as well miserably unliving;
Totally bereft I too am totally absent,
    Appearing here, although
Bruisable and buriable seeming, am too bruised
    In my dead
    Too buried.

329

Spectre who spreads
Internal dissension,
Dividing the unit army of the body
To coward forces,
Since I have brought
To these private places
Sick with his not being, with his recalled
Reverberant fleet blooms of doing and coming,
Empty with his going, since accompanied, entertained,
Shown choicest hothouse blossoms, phenomenal
Plants he acted on to the air like dances lasting,
Since he is not here but where you know with doom!

IV

Where wander those once known herons
Or rabbits here
With shattered entrapped forepaws pitiable in crimson
Killing have known,
And seven-year-old boys locked among ominous
Shadows, enveloped
Have known, and see
As the unmerciful onrush of determined seas
Gathers small craft
There the acquainted faces of the dead sailors
Sight that sees
Where those once known herons fled in fear, to where I
Like lonely herons
The abandoned heroine

V

Go. With mild gradual descent
Burden the memory
Not as he fell, in anger, in the combat

With forms invisible intactual fought
On that mortal rooftop: not with celestial
Speed brought down, in meritorious
Defeat no beating, but like lamed
Herons or birds in wounded slope
Descending down to lamentable homes
In scraggy graves, borne down by death, I come
Drawn down to earth, and underneath
The earth, like one drawn under
Lethal water by an unknown weight
Unseen invisible, but not unknown is fear.

THE CHEMISTRY OF LOVE

The circles and the dreams and the flowering
Clouds, moving like clouds and dreams over
The cumulus, seem to suspend
Twisting wind chains up which to ascend
Like Indian boys into cerulean towers.

Careering like foam mares, leap
The dreams cry, the crystal spine and speed
Sheering the Sun-Moon. Lie here murmur
The flower-clouds, down in the down of the foam
Downs; sink, Anadyomene, into the heavenly
Churning seas, and subside.

Living among the circles and the flowering
Clouds and the dreams of a more real living,
Vital with the circles' and the flowers'
Encircling brilliantly flowering overhead,
Turn then to Love
In whose forever fresh streams
Lies room for the tired limbs' resting,

Enmeshed with flowers and refreshed with
Perennial red showers,
Turning to Love
The flowering circles, the encircling flowers.

Down rainbow veins the blood
Receiving the flower clouds and the circle
Dreams (the streams of rain replenishing
The streams) transmutes those visions to the blood
Of Love, so that one wandering
Among the morning mountains
Following darkly the dreams of circles
Flowers, suffers in blood as rivers
Under red showers, so from his wrist later springs
The rainbowing fountains in whose water circles
Flowers Love soon, and lovelier than all dream.

SUMMER IDYLL

Sometimes in summer months, the gestate earth
Loaded to gold, the boughs arching downward
Burdened, the shallow and glucose streams
Teeming, flowers out, all gold camouflage
Of the collusive summer; but under the streams
Winter lies coldly, and coldly embedded in
The corn hunger lies germinally, want under
The abundance, poverty pulling down
The tautened boughs, and need is the seed.

Robe them in superb summer, at angles
Their bones penetrate, or with a principality
Of Spring possess them, under the breast
Space of a vacancy spreads like a foul
Ghost flower, want; and the pressure upon
The eyeballs of their spirits, upon the organs

Of their spare bodies, the pressure upon
Their movement and their merriment, loving and
Living, the pressure upon their lives like deep
Seas, becomes insufferable, to be suffered.

Sometimes the summer lessens a moment the pressure.
Large as the summer rose some rise
Bathing in rivers or at evening harrying rabbits,
Indulging in games in meadows—and some are idle,
    strewn
Over the parks like soiled paper like summer
Insects, bathed in sweat or at evening harried
By watchmen, park-keepers, policemen—indulge in
    games
Dreaming as I dream of rest and cleanliness and cash.

And the gardens exhibit the regalia of the season
Like debutante queans, between which they wander
Blown with vague odours, seduced by the pure
Beauty, like drowned men floating in bright coral.
Summer, denuding young women, also denudes
Them, removes jackets, exposing backs—
Summer moves many up the river in boats

Trailing their fingers in the shadowed water; they
Too move by the river, and in the water shadows
Trail a hand, which need not find a bank,
Face downward like bad fruit. Cathedrals and Building
Societies, as they appear, disappear; and Beethoven
Is played more loudly to deafen the Welsh echoes,
And Summer, blowing over the Mediterranean
Like swans, like perfect swans.

DYLAN THOMAS

'THE FORCE THAT THROUGH THE GREEN FUSE DRIVES THE FLOWER'

The force that through the green fuse drives the
    flower
Drives my green age; that blasts the roots of trees
Is my destroyer.
And I am dumb to tell the crooked rose
My youth is bent by the same wintry fever.

The force that drives the water through the rocks
Drives my red blood; that dries the mouthing streams
Turns mine to wax.
And I am dumb to mouth unto my veins
How at the mountain spring the same mouth sucks.

The hand that whirls the water in the pool
Stirs the quicksand; that ropes the blowing wind
Hauls my shroud sail.
And I am dumb to tell the hanging man
How of my clay is made the hangman's lime.

The lips of time leech to the fountain head;
Love drips and gathers, but the fallen blood
Shall calm her sores.
And I am dumb to tell a weather's wind
How time has ticked a heaven round the stars.

And I am dumb to tell the lover's tomb
How at my sheet goes the same crooked worm.

'LIGHT BREAKS WHERE NO SUN SHINES' DYLAN
THOMAS

Light breaks where no sun shines;
Where no sea runs, the waters of the heart
Push in their tides;
And, broken ghosts with glowworms in their heads,
The things of light
File through the flesh where no flesh decks the bones.

A candle in the thighs
Warms youth and seed and burns the seeds of age;
Where no seed stirs,
The fruit of man unwrinkles in the stars,
Bright as a fig;
Where no wax is, the candle shows its hairs.

Dawn breaks behind the eyes;
From poles of skull and toe the windy blood
Slides like a sea;
Nor fenced, nor staked, the gushers of the sky
Spout to the rod
Divining in a smile the oil of tears.

Night in the sockets rounds,
Like some pitch moon, the limit of the globes;
Day lights the bone;
Where no cold is, the skinning gales unpin
The winter's robes;
The film of spring is hanging from the lids.

Light breaks on secret lots,
On tips of thought where thoughts smell in the rain;
When logics die,
The secret of the soil grows through the eye,
And blood jumps in the sun;
Above the waste allotments the dawn halts.

CLIFFORD DYMENT

A SWITCH CUT IN APRIL

This thin elastic stick was plucked
From gradual growing in a hedge,
Where early mist awakened leaf
And late damp hands with spiral stroke
Smoothed slumber from the weighted day
While flowers drooped with colours furled.

I cut quick circles with the stick:
It whistles in the April air
An eager song, a bugle call,
A signal for the running feet,
For rising flyer flashing sun,
And windy tree with surging crest.

This pliant wood like expert whip
Snaps action in its voice, commands
A quiver from the sloth, achieves
A jerk in buds; with stinging lash
A spring of movement in the stiff
And sleeping limbs of winter land.

Stick plucked and peeled, companions lost,
Torn from its rooted stock: I hold
Elate and lithe within my hand
Winged answer to the wings' impulse,
The calyx breaking into flame,
The crystal cast into the light.

THE PASSION

CLIFFORD
DYMENT

Image of the rose, of roses,
In this closed soil where
The suck and the roar of streets
Sounds like a sea.

Image of the rose, of roses,
Curling in this dry land:
Here is no cactus;
There is no fountain tossing
In shining showers;
No brooks are sparkling in the rocks.

Image of the rose, of roses,
Red of the glittering armies,
And the towers, the walls, falling.
The guerdon of the handsome horseman
Triumphant in trumpets and colours;
Splendid mirror of lovers' lips.

O rose, O thirsty roses,
Red of the crown, of the agony;
Flower of blood upon the brow,
And wings falling shot from flight.

Image of the rose, of roses,
Bright is the light burning
The weary, the wise, the sorrowful eyes.

FOX

Exploiter of the shadows
He moved among the fences,
A strip of action coiling
Around his farmyard fancies.

With shouting fields are shaken,
The spinneys give no shelter;
There is delight for riders,
For hounds a tooth in shoulder.

The creature tense with wildness
Knows death is sudden falling
From fury into weary
Surrendering of feeling.

DAVID GASCOYNE

LANDSCAPE

Across the correct perspective to the painted sky
Scores of reflected bridges merging
One into the other pass, and crowds with flags
Rush over them, and clouds like acrobats
Swing on an invisible trapeze.

The light like a sharpened pencil
Writes histories of darkness on the wall,
While walls fall inwards, septic wounds
Burst open like sewn mouths, and rain
Eternally descends through planetary space.

We ask: Whence comes this light?
Whence comes the rain, the planetary
Silences, these aqueous monograms
Of our unique and isolated selves?
Only a dusty statue lifts and drops its hand.

IN DEFENCE OF HUMANISM

To M. Salvador Dali

The face of the precipice is black with lovers;
The sun above them is a bag of nails; the spring's
First rivers hide among their hair.
Goliath plunges his hand into the poisoned well
And bows his head and feels my feet walk through his
    brain.
The children chasing butterflies turn round and see him
    there,

With his hand in the well and my body growing from
his head,
And are afraid. They drop their nets and walk into the
wall like smoke.

The smooth plain with its rivers listens to the cliff
Like a basilisk eating flowers.
And the children, lost in the shadows of the catacombs,
Call to the mirrors for help:
'Strong-bow of salt, cutlass of memory,
Write on my map the name of every river.'

A flock of banners fight their way through the
telescoped forest
And fly away like birds towards the sound of roasting
meat.
Sand falls into the boiling rivers through the
telescopes' mouths
And forms clear drops of acid with petals of whirling
flame.
Heraldic animals wade through the asphyxia of planets,
Butterflies burst from their skins and grow long
tongues like plants,
The plants play games with a suit of mail like a cloud.

Mirrors write Goliath's name upon my forehead,
While the children are killed in the smoke of the
catacombs
And lovers float down from the cliff like rain.

THE SUPPOSED BEING

DAVID GAS-
COYNE

Supposing the mouth
the hard lips crowned with bright flowers
a bursting foam of petals
and each gold stamen an anxious arrow
as each firm finger a signal
pointing to fire and water's junction
whose furious fumes would stifle the passers-by
with their startled eyes
with their nervous hands and faces
whose language is black whose language has
never been ours.

Supposing the eyes
luscious in lashes and deep stained with sleep
the eyes in the forehead like pools in the rocks
and the turbulent sea approaching
shivering ravenous venomous—scarred
by the sharp-taloned claws of its waves
as eyes by their ravaging lids
as their lids by the richly veined hands
that are burnt by the light of the sun
and the stones are on fire
and the pupils of eyes are glazed by the
heat of their flames.

Supposing the hands
with their nails and their delicate bones
like the frail limbs of birds
and their tips like the pink tips of buds
that probe the cold curious air
and discover the blood neath the skin
and the surface of stones.

DAVID Supposing the breasts
GAS- like shells on the oceanless shore
COYNE at the end of the world
like furious thrusts of a single knife
like bread to be broken by hands
supposing the breasts still untouched by desires
still unsuckled by thirsts
and motionless still
·breasts violently still and enisled in the
night and afraid both of love and of death.

Supposing the sex
a cruelty and dread in the thighs
a gaping and blackness—a charred
trace of feverish flames
the sex like an X
as the sign and the imprint of all that has gone before
as a torch
to enlighten the forests of gloom and the
mountains of unattained night.

And supposing the being entire
the tangible body standing
the visible limbs existing
and moving across the daylight
or motionless in the darkness
a stone on the torrent's bed
or a torrent above the stones—
and at last
such a being escapes from the sight of my visible eyes
from the touch of my tangible hands
for she only exists
where all contradictions exist
where darkness is light and the real is unreal and the
world is a dream in a dream.

ACKNOWLEDGEMENTS

ACKNOWLEDGEMENTS

For permission to reprint copyright material, the following acknowledgements are made:

For poems by Gerard Manley Hopkins, to the poet's family and the Oxford University Press.
> *Poems: Edited by Robert Bridges.* Second Edition (O.U.P.) 1930.

For poems by W. B. Yeats, to the author and Messrs. Macmillan & Co.
> *Collected Poems* (Macmillan) 1933.

For poems by T. E. Hulme, to Mr. Herbert Read and Messrs. Kegan Paul, Trench, Trübner & Co.
> *Speculations* (Kegan Paul) 1924. Hulme's five poems had previously been printed as an addendum to Ezra Pound's *Ripostes* (Elkin Mathews).

For poems by Ezra Pound, to the author and to Messrs. Faber & Faber.
> *Selected Poems* (Faber) 1928.
> *Homage to Sextus Propertius* (Faber) 1934.
> *A Draft of XXX Cantos* (Faber) 1933.

For poems by T. S. Eliot, to the author and to Messrs. Faber & Faber.
> *Collected Poems 1909-1935* (Faber) 1936

For poems by Harold Monro, to Mrs. Alida Monro and Mr. Cobden-Sanderson.
> *Collected Poems* (Cobden-Sanderson) 1933.

For poems by Conrad Aiken, to the author and Charles Scribner's Sons.
> *Preludes for Memnon* (Scribners) 1931.

For poems by H.D., to Mrs. H. D. Aldington, Mr. Horace Liveright and Messrs. Chatto & Windus.

Collected Poems (Boni & Liveright) 1925.

Red Roses for Bronze (Chatto & Windus) 1931.

For poems by Marianne Moore, to the author and Messrs. Faber & Faber.

Selected Poems (Faber) 1935.

For poems by Wallace Stevens, to the author and Mr. Alfred Knopf.

Harmonium (Knopf) 1931.

For the poem by Vachel Lindsay, to Mrs. Lindsay and The Macmillan Company.

Collected Poems (Macmillan) 1922.

For poems by D. H. Lawrence, to Mrs. Frieda Lawrence, Messrs. Heinemann and Mr. Martin Secker.

Collected Poems (Secker) 1932.

Last Poems (Secker) 1933.

For poems by Isaac Rosenberg, to Mrs. I. Wynick and Messrs. Chatto & Windus.

Poems (Chatto & Windus) 1936.

For poems by Wilfred Owen, to Mrs. Susan Owen and Messrs. Chatto & Windus.

Poems (Chatto & Windus) 1931.

For poems by Herbert Read, to the author and Messrs. Faber & Faber.

Collected Poems (Faber) 1935.

For poems by John Crowe Ransom, to the author, the Hogarth Press and Mr. Alfred Knopf.

Grace after Meat (Hogarth Press) 1924.

Chills and Fever (Knopf) 1924.

Two Gentlemen in Bonds (Knopf) 1927.

For poems by Allen Tate, to the author, Minton, Balch & Co., and Charles Scribner's Sons.

Mr. Pope and Other Poems (Minton, Balch & Co.) 1928.

Poems 1928-1931 (Scribners) 1931.

'The Mediterranean' appeared in *New Verse* (October 1933)

For poems by Hart Crane, to the poet's family and Mr. Horace Liveright.

Collected Poems (Liveright) 1933.

For poems by E. E. Cummings, to the author and Mr. Horace Liveright.

is 5 (Boni & Liveright) 1926.

For poems by Laura Riding, to the author, the Seizin Press, and Mr. Arthur Barker.

Poems: A Joking Word (Cape) 1930. (*Out of print.*)

Poet: A Lying Word (Barker) 1933.

'Auspice of Jewels' has not previously been printed.

For poems by Robert Graves, to the author and the Seizin Press.

Poems 1926-1930 (Heinemann) 1931.

Poems 1930-1933 (Barker) 1933.

'To bring the Dead to Life' has not previously been printed.

For poems by Edith Sitwell, to the author, Mr. Basil Blackwell and Messrs. Duckworth & Co.

The Wooden Pegasus (Blackwell) 1920.

Collected Poems (Duckworth) 1930.

For poems by Sacheverell Sitwell, to the author and Messrs. Faber & Faber.

Canons of Giant Art (Faber) 1933.

For the poem by Richard Eberhart, to the author.

'The Groundhog' appeared in *Poems of Tomorrow* (Chatto & Windus) 1935.

For poems by Peter Quennell, to the author and Messrs. Chatto & Windus.

Poems (Chatto & Windus) 1926.

For poems by William Empson, to the author and Messrs. Chatto & Windus.

Poems (Chatto & Windus) 1935.

For poems by C. Day Lewis, to the author and the Hogarth Press.

Collected Poems (Hogarth Press) 1935.

A Time to Dance (Hogarth Press) 1935.

For poems by W. H. Auden, to the author and Messrs. Faber & Faber.

Poems: Revised Edition (Faber) 1933.

The Orators (Faber) 1932.

'Prologue' appeared in *New Country* (Hogarth Press) 1933.

'Our Hunting Fathers' and 'A Bride in the '30's' appeared in *Poems of Tomorrow* (Chatto & Windus) 1935.

For poems by Louis MacNeice, to the author and Messrs. Faber & Faber.

Poems (Faber) 1935.

For poems by Stephen Spender, to the author and Messrs. Faber & Faber.

> *Poems: Revised Edition* (Faber) 1934.
> 'The North' appeared in *Poems of Tomorrow* (Chatto & Windus) 1935.
> 'An Elementary School Classroom' and 'Exiles' appeared in *The London Mercury* (May 1935).
> 'The Uncreating Chaos' appeared in *New Verse* (October 1935).

For poems by James Reeves, to the author, to the Seizin Press and to Messrs. Constable & Co.

> *The Natural Need* (Seizin Press and Constable & Co.) 1935.

For poems by Charles Madge, to the author.

> 'Blocking the Pass', 'Fortune', 'Loss' and 'Solar Creation' appeared in *Poems of Tomorrow* (Chatto & Windus) 1935.
> 'Lusty Juventus', 'At War' and 'The Hours of the Planets' appeared in *New Verse* (August and December 1934).
> 'In Conjunction' and 'A Monument' appeared in *The Criterion* (July 1934).

For poems by George Barker, to the author, the Parton Press and Messrs. Faber & Faber.

> *Thirty Preliminary Poems* (Parton Press) 1933.
> *Poems* (Faber) 1935.
> 'The Chemistry of Love' and 'Summer Idyll' have not previously been printed.

For poems by Dylan Thomas, to the author, to the *Sunday Referee* and to Parton Press.

> *18 Poems* (Sunday Referee and Parton Press) 1934.

For poems by Clifford Dyment, to the author.

'A Switch Cut in April' appeared in *The Year's Poetry*, 1935 (Bodley Head).

'Fox' appeared in *Poems of Tomorrow* (Chatto & Windus) 1935.

'The Passion' has not previously been printed.

For poems by David Gascoyne, to the author.

'Landscape' appeared in *The Year's Poetry* (Bodley Head) 1934.

'In Defence of Humanism' appeared in *The New Republic* (October 17, 1934).

'The Supposed Being' has not previously been printed.

INDEX OF AUTHORS

Roberts, Michael, ed.
   The Faber book of modern verse.   London,
Faber and Faber [1936]
   352p. 19cm.